Praise for *Shadow Government*

"This is a book about secrets and surveillance, but I'm here to tell you one secret its contents won't. For more than a dozen years, Tom Engelhardt and his website or blog or post-newspaper wire service Tomdispatch.com have been one of the great forces on the side of clarity, democracy, openness, and really good writing. Tom himself, a legendary book editor, is also one of the country's most eloquent and tenacious political writers, electronically publishing three essays a week for all these years and writing many of them himself. This collection, focused on the new Orwellianism, is some of the finest writing and finest public service gathered together in book form for your portable pleasure and outrage."
—Rebecca Solnit, author of *Men Explain Things to Me*

"Tom Engelhardt is an iconoclast, but he also is the latest exemplar of a great American tradition. Like George Seldes and I. F. Stone before him, he has bypassed conventionally minded newspapers and magazines and, with his remarkable website and in books like this, found a way of addressing readers directly about the issues central to our time. Again and again, he goes to the heart of the matter, drawing on his awesomely wide reading, his knowledge of history, and his acute political radar system that uncovers small but deeply revealing nuggets of news and often makes me feel, enviously: How could I have missed that?"
—Adam Hochschild, author of *King Leopold's Ghost*

"Tom Engelhardt's writing on the new forms of government surveillance is crucial because he has spent a lifetime studying the rise of the national security state. He can therefore put the contemporary practices of the National Security Agency and the destruction of the Fourth Amendment in the context of the rise of a twenty-first-century Leviathan that he has chronicled for us for decades. As we arrive a few decades late at Orwell's *1984*, Tom Engelhardt is our anti–Winston Smith, writing the newspaper articles back into their original form and washing out the propaganda."
—Juan Cole, Richard P. Mitchell Collegiate Professor of History at the University of Michigan

Praise for *The United States of Fear*

"Tom Engelhardt, as always, focuses his laser-like intelligence on a core problem that the media avoid: Obama's stunning embrace of Bush's secret government by surveillance, torture, and sanctioned assassination. A stunning polemic."
—Mike Davis, author of *In Praise of Barbarians* and *Planet of Slums*

Praise for *The American Way of War*

"A tour de force."

—Jeremy Scahill, author of *Blackwater*

"There are a lot of ways to describe Tom Engelhardt's astonishing service to this country's conscience and imagination: you could portray him as our generation's Orwell, standing aside from all conventional framings to see afresh our dilemmas and blind spots, as the diligent little boy sending in regular dispatches on the nakedness of the emperor and his empire, as a Bodhisattva dedicated to saving all beings through compassion and awareness, but analogies don't really describe the mix of clear and sometimes hilarious writing, deep insight, superb information, empathy, and outrage that has been the core of Tom's TomDispatches for almost a decade, or the extraordinary contribution they've made to the American dialogue. Check out this bundle of some of the best from that time span."

—Rebecca Solnit, author of *Men Explain Things to Me*

"They may have Blackwater/Xe, Halliburton, aircraft carrier battle groups, deadly drones by the score, and the world's largest military budget, but *we* have Tom Engelhardt—and a more powerful truth-seeking missile has seldom been invented. Longtime fans like me will be happy to see some of his most memorable pieces reprinted here, although woven together in a way that makes them still stronger; for anyone not yet familiar with his work, this is your chance to meet one of the most forceful analysts alive of our country's dangerous, costly addiction to all things military."

—Adam Hochschild, author of *King Leopold's Ghost*

"Tom Engelhardt is the I. F. Stone of the post–9/11 age—seeing what others miss, calling attention to contradictions that others willfully ignore, insisting that Americans examine in full precisely those things that make us most uncomfortable."

—Andrew J. Bacevich, author of *Washington Rules*

"Tom Engelhardt is among our most trenchant critics of American perpetual war. Like I. F. Stone in the 1960s, he has an uncanny ability to ferret out and see clearly the ugly truths hidden in government reports and statistics. No cynic, he always measures the sordid reality against a bright vision of an America that lives up to its highest ideals."

—Juan Cole, Richard P. Mitchell Collegiate Professor of History at the University of Michigan

"Like an extended Motown shuffle with some hard-hitting Stax breaks, and never devoid of an all too human sense of humor and pathos, Tom's book takes us for the ride. And though the landscape surveyed is all too familiar for anyone who has followed George 'Dubya's' wars, it ain't pretty; and it does lead to a black hole in our collective soul. . . . [I]nvaluable in showing how the empire walks the walk and talks the talk."

—Pepe Escobar, *Asia Times*

"If a person could approach you on the street, gently caress your cheek, and walk away leaving you with the feeling of having been violently slapped and dowsed with a bucket of ice water, they would approximate Tom Engelhardt's writing, including that in his newest book *The American Way of War: How Bush's Wars Became Obama's*....What Engelhardt has written over the past several years and collected here on the subject of war needed to be said and will continue to need to be said more loudly with each passing day."

—David Swanson, Fire Dog Lake

"In *The American Way of War: How Bush's Wars Became Obama's* (Haymarket Books, 2010), Tom Engelhardt provides a clear-eyed examination of U.S. foreign policy in the Bush and Obama years, and details unsparingly how Obama has inherited—and in many cases exacerbated—the ills of the Bush era. . . . an important book for anyone hoping to understand how the U.S. arrived at its current predicament during the Bush years, and how it remains in this predicament despite Obama's best efforts—or perhaps because of them."

—Inter Press Service

"Tom Engelhardt's biting look at United States militarism, *The American Way of War: How Bush's Wars Became Obama's* . . . [is] pithy . . . [and] alarming. . . . He takes on our war-possessed world with clear-eyed, penetrating precision."

—*Mother Jones Online*

"Essential. . . . seamlessly edited. . . . establishes him as one of the grand chroniclers of the post–9/11 era."

—Dan Froomkin, Nieman Watchdog

"These simple pleas for readers to reconsider an idea they might previously have taken for granted are one of the strengths of this book. Demonstrating Engelhardt's experience as a professional editor, he avoids the overly strident or self-righteous condescension that characterizes too much online political writing, instead using clear and unvarnished prose to attack the fundamental principles of the post–September 11 mindset."

—*Foreign Policy in Focus*

"American history does not begin with 9/11, yet the worldview of so many in the United States since then has been shaped by how the mainstream media had coloured events following the terrorist attacks. But to break free from that distorted perception which bears little resemblance to reality—as people once knew it—one needs the help of a little imagination. In Tom Engelhardt's *The American Way of War: How Bush's Wars Became Obama's*, you could step back and see all the views that you had taken for granted challenged, as you indulge yourself in a world of ideas that are logical and straightforward but just were not quite visible to you before. All of course are backed by key facts, sound analysis and invaluable context."

—Middle East Online

"With an excellent mind and an equally fine pen, Engelhardt demonstrates true patriotism to the American founding. . . . Reading such good prose invigorates like little else in this world of sorrows. But one should not consider Engelhardt merely a writer of golden prose. This body has a soul as well, and Engelhardt convincingly presents evidence as well as argument throughout the book. . . . *The American Way of War* is brimming with insights."

—The American Conservative

"Excellent. . . . Anyone who wants to rebuild an antiwar movement . . . should read *The American Way of War*. . . . Reading this book feels like poking around with a flashlight in the unexamined corners of the post–9/11 American imperial mindset. . . . sharp wit runs throughout the book. The section about the lack of media coverage of air campaigns, for example, is wonderfully titled 'On Not Looking Up.' Not only does this humor make *The American Way of War* a surprisingly entertaining read given the subject matter, it reminds us of something all great antiwar movements have known—the war machine is not just evil, it's often absurd."

—Socialist Worker

Praise for TomDispatch

"One of my favorite websites"

—Bill Moyers

"At a time when the mainstream media leave out half of what the public needs to know, while at the same time purveying oceans of official nonsense, the public needs an alternative source of news. Tom Engelhardt's TomDispatch has been that for me. With unerring touch, he finds the stories I need to read, prefacing them each day with introductions that in themselves form a witty, hugely enjoyable, brilliant running commentary on the times. He is my mainstream."

—Jonathan Schell

"Tom Engelhardt is a national treasure and always worth reading. Whenever I think that Russell Jacoby might have been right about the passing of the 'last intellectuals,' I think of Tom and conclude, 'not yet.'"

—Juan Cole, Richard P. Mitchell Collegiate Professor of History at the University of Michigan

"Tom Engelhardt [is] a writer of titanic energy and commitment."

—James Wolcott

"Tom Engelhardt [is] the finest and hardest-working essayist and editor of the post–9/11 era, who has kept a steady eye on Washington's 'baser' intentions since even before the 2003 invasion."

—Jim Lobe, Inter Press Service, at his Lobelog blog

"Indispensable."

—Tony Karon

Praise for *The World According to TomDispatch*

"These are the traits of a TomDispatch essay: unapologetically intellectual, relentlessly original, a little bit dangerous. For many of us, these are the key pieces of analysis that made sense of our post–9/11 world. How odd that many of them have never actually been printed. Until now."

—Naomi Klein

"At a time when the fourth estate so often seems to be in its death throes, it's our great good fortune to have TomDispatch, where vital and independent commentary abounds and the provocative ideas of genuine public intellectuals are given full rein."

—Susan Faludi

"TomDispatch is one of the wonders of the electronic age. A touch of the finger and you get the juiciest, meatiest information and analysis, so rich a feast of intelligence and insight I often felt short of breath. Now, Tom Engelhardt has assembled some of the best of his dispatches, from some of the boldest and most astute commentators in the country. So take a deep breath and read."

—Howard Zinn

"TomDispatch is essential reading. It is a one-stop shop where you can find the most provocative thinkers writing the most eloquent and hard-hitting articles about the most pressing issues of the day. Read, get mad, and take action."

—Amy Goodman

Shadow Government

Surveillance, Secret Wars, and a Global Security State in a Single-Superpower World

TOM ENGELHARDT

Haymarket Books
Chicago, Illinois

Published in 2014 by Haymarket Books
PO Box 180165
Chicago, IL 60618
www.haymarketbooks.org
773-583-7884
info@haymarketbooks.org

ISBN: 978-1-60846-365-7

Trade distribution:
In the US, Consortium Book Sales and Distribution, www.cbsd.com
In Canada, Publishers Group Canada, www.pgcbooks.ca
In the UK, Turnaround Publisher Services, www.turnaround-uk.com
All other countries, Publishers Group Worldwide, www.pgw.com

Cover design by Eric Ruder. Cover photo of the headquarters of the National Security
Agency by Trevor Paglen. From *The Intercept.*

Published with the generous support of Lannan Foundation
and the Wallace Action Fund.

Printed in Canada by union labor.

Library of Congress cataloging-in-publication data is available.

10 9 8 7 6 5 4 3 2

CONTENTS

FOREWORD   by Glenn Greenwald   1

ONE   The Shadow Government's Secret Religion   3

TWO   How the US Intelligence Community
                    Came Out of the Shadows   17

THREE   How to Be a Rogue Superpower   29

FOUR   Mistaking Omniscience for Omnipotence   43

FIVE   Definitions for a New Age   61

SIX   Why Washington Can't Stop   91

SEVEN   Overwrought Empire   109

EIGHT   The Obama Contradiction   127

NINE   Destroying the Planet for Record Profits   137

TEN   A Golden Age for Journalism   149

AFTERWORD   Letter to an Unknown Whistleblower   157

Acknowledgments   163

A Note on the Text   165

Index   167

For Charlie:
May you live in a world where you can be seen
but not surveilled.

FOREWORD

It was more than a year ago that I was first contacted by National Security Agency whistleblower Edward Snowden. He contacted me by email. He was anonymous. I had no idea who he was. He didn't say much. He simply said he had what he thought would be some documents I would be interested in looking at, which turned out to be the world's largest understatement of the decade.

When I asked Snowden how he got himself to the point where he was willing to take the risk that he knew he was taking, he told me that for a long time he had been looking for a leader, somebody who would come and fix these problems. And then one day he realized that there's no point in waiting for a leader, that leadership is about going first and about setting an example for others. He decided he simply didn't want to live in a world where the US government was permitted to have such extraordinary powers and to build a system that had as its goal the destruction of all individual privacy—that he could not in good conscience stand by and allow that to happen knowing that he had the power to help stop it.

The goal of the US surveillance state is to make sure that there is no such thing as actual human privacy, not just in the United States but in the world. That's its intent. It does that by design. What we are really talking about is a globalized system that prevents any form of electronic communication from taking place without being stored and monitored by

1

the National Security Agency. It's not just journalists but also dissident groups and Muslim communities that have been infiltrated and monitored. The government is deliberately working to create a climate of fear in exactly those communities that are most important in checking those in power.

I really don't think there's any more important battle today than combating the surveillance state. Ultimately, the thing that matters most is that the rights that we know we have as human beings are rights that we exercise. The only way those rights can ever be taken away is if we give in to the fear that is being deliberately imposed on our world. You can acculturate people to believing that tyranny is freedom, and that as a consequence their limits are actually liberties. That is what this surveillance state does, by training people to accept their own conformity so they no longer even realize the ways in which they're being limited.

As Rosa Luxemburg once said, "He who does not move does not notice his chains." The point of Tom Engelhardt's important work at TomDispatch.com and in *Shadow Government* is to help us find the way to break those chains.

—Glenn Greenwald

ONE

The Shadow Government's Secret Religion

In a 1950s civics textbook of mine, I can remember a Martian landing on Main Street, USA, to be instructed in the glories of our political system. You know, our tripartite government, checks and balances, a miraculous set of rights, and vibrant democracy. There was, Americans then thought, much to be proud of, and so for that generation of schoolchildren, many Martians were instructed in the American way of life. These days, I suspect, not so many.

Still, I wondered just what lessons might be offered to such a Martian crash-landing in Washington today. Certainly checks, balances, rights, and democracy wouldn't top any list. Since my childhood, in fact, that tripartite government has grown a fourth part, a national security state that is remarkably unchecked and unbalanced. In recent times, that labyrinthine structure—of intelligence agencies morphing into warfighting outfits, the US military (with its own secret military, the special operations forces, gestating inside it), and the Department of Homeland Security (DHS), a monster conglomeration of agencies that is an actual "defense department," as well as a vast contingent of weapons makers, contractors, and profiteers bolstered by an army of lobbyists—has never stopped growing. It has won the undying fealty of Congress, embraced the power of the presidency, made itself into a jobs program for the

American people, and been largely free to do as it pleased with almost unlimited taxpayer dollars.

The expansion of Washington's national security state—let's call it the NSS—to gargantuan proportions has historically met with little opposition. In the wake of the Edward Snowden revelations, however, some resistance has arisen, especially when it comes to the "right" of one part of the NSS to turn the world into a listening post in order to gather, in particular, American communications of every sort. The debate about this—invariably framed as whether or not we should have more security or more privacy and how exactly to balance the two—has been reasonably vigorous. The problem is: it doesn't begin to get at the real nature of the NSS or the dangers it poses.

If I were to instruct that stray Martian lost in the nation's capital, I might choose another framework entirely for my lesson. After all, the focus of the NSS, which has like an incubus grown to monstrous size inside the body of the political system, would seem distinctly monomaniacal, if only we could step outside our normal way of thinking for a moment. At a cost of nearly a trillion dollars a year, its main global enemy consists of thousands of lightly armed jihadis and wannabe jihadis scattered mainly across the backlands of the planet. They are capable of causing genuine damage—though far less to the United States than to numerous other countries—but not of shaking our way of life. And yet for the leaders, bureaucrats, corporate cronies, rank and file, and acolytes of the NSS, it's a focus that can never be intense enough on behalf of a system that can never grow large enough or be well funded enough.

None of the frameworks we normally call on to understand the NSS capture the irrationality, genuine inanity, and actual madness that lie at its heart. Perhaps reimagining what has developed in these last decades as a faith-based system—a new national religion—would help. This, at least, is the way I would try to explain the latest version of Washington to that wayward Martian.

Holy Warriors

Imagine what we call "national security" as, at its core, a proselytizing warrior religion. It has its holy orders. It has its sacred texts (classified).

It has its dogma and its warrior priests. It has its sanctified promised land, known as "the homeland." It has its seminaries, which we call think tanks. It is a monotheistic faith in that it broaches no alternatives to itself. It is Manichaean in its view of the world. As with so many religions, its god is an eye in the sky, an all-seeing being who knows your secrets.

Edward Snowden, the man who in 2013 pulled back the curtain on part of this system, revealing its true nature to anyone who cared to look, is an apostate, never to be forgiven by those in its holy orders. He is a Judas to be hunted down, returned to the United States, put on trial as a "traitor," and then—so say some retired NSS warriors (who often channel the opinions and feelings of those still in office)—hung by the neck until dead or swung "from a tall oak tree."

Al-Qaeda is, of course, the system's Devil, whose evil seed is known to land and breed anywhere on the planet, from Sana'a, Yemen, to Boston, Massachusetts, if we are not eternally and ever more on guard. In the name of the epic global struggle against it and the need to protect the homeland, nothing is too much, no step taken a point too far. (As the Devil is traditionally a shape-shifter, able to manifest himself in many forms, it is possible that tomorrow's version of him may be, say, Russia or China.)

The leaders of this faith-based system are, not surprisingly, fundamentalist true believers. They don't wear long beards, wave the Koran, shout "Death to the Great Satan," or live in the backlands of the planet. Instead, they speak bureaucratically, tend to sport military uniforms and medals, and inhabit high-tech government facilities. Fundamentalist as they are, they may not, in the normal sense, be religious at all. They are not obliged to believe in the importance of being "born again" or fear being "left behind" in a future "end times"—though such beliefs don't disqualify them either.

They issue the equivalent of fatwas against those they proclaim to be their enemies. They have a set of Sharia-like laws, both immutable and flexible. Punishments for breaking them may not run to death by stoning or the cutting off of hands, but they do involve the cutting off of lives.

Theirs is an implacable warrior religion, calling down retribution on people often seen only poorly by video feed, thousands of miles from Washington, DC, Langley, Virginia, or Fort Meade, Maryland. It's no mistake that the weapons fired by their fleet of drone aircraft are called Hellfire missiles, since it is indeed hellfire and brimstone that they believe they are delivering to the politically sinful of the world. Nor is it a happenstance that the planes firing those missiles have been dubbed Predators and Reapers (as in "grim"), for they do see themselves as the anointed deliverers of death to their enemies.

While they have a powerful urge to maintain the faith the American public has in them, they also believe deeply that they know best, that their knowledge is the Washington equivalent of God-given, and that the deepest mysteries and secrets of their religion should be held close indeed.

Unless you enter their orders and rise into their secret world, there is such a thing as too much knowledge. As a result, they have developed a faith-based system of secrecy in which the deepest mysteries have, until recently, been held by the smallest numbers of believers, in which disputes are adjudicated in a "court" system so secret that only favored arguments by the NSS can be presented to its judges, in which just about any document produced, no matter how anodyne, will be classified as too dangerous to be read by "the people." This has meant that, until recently, most assessments of the activities of the NSS have had to be taken on faith.

In addition, in the service of that faith, NSS officials may—and their religion permits this—lie to and manipulate the public, Congress, allies, or anyone else, and do so without compunction. They may publicly deny realities they know to exist, or offer, as Conor Friedersdorf of the *Atlantic* has written, statements "exquisitely crafted to mislead." They do this based on the belief that the deepest secrets of their world and its operations can only truly be understood by those already inducted into their orders. And yet they are not simply manipulating us in service to their One True Faith. Nothing is ever that simple. Before they manipulate us, they must spend years manipulating themselves. Only because they have already convinced themselves of the deeper truth of their mission do they accept the necessity of manipulating others in what still passes for a democracy. To serve the people, in other words, they have no choice but to lie to them.

Like other religious institutions in their heyday, the NSS has shown a striking ability to generate support for its ever-growing structure by turning itself into a lucrative global operation. In a world where genuine enemies are in remarkably short supply (though you'd never know it from the Gospel according to the NSS), it has exhibited remarkable skill in rallying those who might support it financially, whether they call themselves Democrats or Republicans, and ensuring, even in budgetary tough times, that its coffers will continue to burst at the seams.

It has also worked hard to expand what, since 1961, has been known as the military-industrial complex. In the twenty-first century, the NSS has put special effort into subsidizing warrior corporations ready to join it on the global battlefield. In the process, it has privatized—that is, corporatized—its global operations. It has essentially merged with a set of crony outfits that now do a significant part of its work. It has hired contractors by the tens of thousands, creating corporate spies, corporate analysts, corporate mercenaries, corporate builders, and corporate providers for a structure that is increasingly becoming the profit-center of a state within a state. All of this, in turn, helps to support a growing theocratic warrior class in the luxury to which it has become accustomed.

Since 9/11, the result has been a religion of perpetual conflict whose doctrines tend to grow ever more extreme. In our time, for instance, the NSS has moved from Dick Cheney's "1 percent doctrine" (if there's even a 1 percent chance that some country might someday attack us, we should "act as if it is a certainty") to something like a "zero percent doctrine." Whether in its drone wars with presidential "kill lists" or the cyberwar— probably the first in history—that it launched against Iran, it no longer cares to argue most of the time that such strikes need even a 1 percent justification. Its ongoing, self-proclaimed Global War on Terror, whether on the ground or in the air, in person or by drone, in space or cyberspace (where its newest military command is already in action) is justification enough for just about any act, however aggressive.

Put all this together and what you have is a description of a militant organization whose purpose is to carry out a Washington-based version of global jihad, a perpetual war in the name of the true faith.

A Practical Failure, a Faith-Based Success Story

Looked at another way, the NSS is also a humongous humbug, a gigantic fraud of a belief system that only delivers because its followers never choose to look at the world through Martian eyes.

Let's start with its gargantuan side. No matter how you cut it, the NSS is a Ripley's Believe It or Not! of staggering numbers that, once you step outside its thought system, don't add up. The US national defense budget is estimated to be larger than those of the next thirteen countries combined—that is, simply off-the-charts more expensive. The US Navy has eleven aircraft carrier strike groups when no other country has more than two. No other national security outfit can claim to sweep up "nearly five billion records a day on the whereabouts of cellphones around the world," or, like the NSA's Special Source Operations group in 2006, boast about being capable of ingesting the equivalent of "one Library of Congress every 14.4 seconds," nor does it have any competitors when it comes to constructing "building complexes for top-secret intelligence work" (thirty-three in the Washington area alone between 2001 and 2010). Its building programs around the United States and globally are never-ending.

It is creating a jet fighter that will be the most expensive weapons system in history. Its weapons makers controlled 78 percent of the global arms market in 2012. When its military departed Iraq after eight years of invasion and occupation, it left with three million objects ranging from armored vehicles to laptop computers and port-a-potties (and destroyed or handed over to the Iraqis countless more). In a world where other countries have, at best, a handful of military bases outside their territories, it has hundreds. In 2011 alone, it managed to classify 92,064,862 of the documents it generated, giving secrecy a new order of magnitude. And that's just to dip a toe in the ocean of a national security state that dwarfs the one that fought the Cold War against an actual imperial superpower.

Again, if you were to step outside the world of NSS dogma and the arguments that go with it, such numbers—and they are legion—would surely represent one of the worst investments in modern memory. If a system of this sort weren't faith-based, and if that faith weren't widespread and deeply accepted (even if now possibly on the wane), people would automatically look at such numbers, compare them to the results, and ask why, for all its promises of safety and security, the NSS so regularly fails to deliver. And why the response to failure can always be encapsulated in one word: more.

After all, if the twenty-first century has taught us anything, it's that the most expensive and over-equipped military on the planet can't win a war. Its two multitrillion-dollar attempts since 9/11, in Iraq and Afghanistan, both against lightly armed minority insurgencies, proved disasters. (In Iraq, however, despite an ignominious US pullout and the chaos that has followed in the region, the NSS and its supporters have continued to promote the idea that General David Petraeus's "surge" was indeed some kind of historic last-minute "victory.")

After twelve long years in Afghanistan and an Obama-era surge in that country, the latest grim National Intelligence Estimate from the US Intelligence Community suggests that no matter what Washington now does, the likelihood is that things there will only go from bad enough to far worse. Years of a drone campaign against al-Qaeda in the Arabian Peninsula have strengthened that organization; an air intervention in Libya led to chaos, a dead ambassador, and a growing al-Qaeda movement in northern Africa—and so it repetitively goes.

Similarly, intelligence officials brag of terrorist plots—fifty-four of them!—that have been broken up thanks in whole or in part to the NSA's metadata sweeps of US phone calls; it also claims that, given the need for secrecy, only four of them can be made public. (The claims of success on even those four, when examined by journalists, have proven less than impressive.) Meanwhile, the presidential task force charged with reviewing the NSA revelations, which had access to a far wider range of insider information, came to an even more startling conclusion: not one instance could be found in which the metadata the NSA was storing in bulk had thwarted a terrorist plot. "Our review," the panel wrote, "suggests that the information contributed to terrorist investigations by the use of section 215 telephony meta-data was not essential to preventing attacks." And keep in mind that, based on what we do know about such terror plots, a surprising number of them were planned, sparked, or made possible by FBI-inspired plants.

In fact, claims of success against such plots couldn't be more faith-based, relying as they generally do on the word of intelligence officials who have proven themselves untrustworthy or on the impossible-to-prove-or-disprove claim that if such a system didn't exist, far worse would have happened. That version of a success story is well summarized in the claim that "we didn't have another 9/11."

In other words, in bang-for-the-buck practical terms, Washington's NSS should be viewed as a remarkable failure. And yet, in faith-based terms, it couldn't be a greater success. Its false gods are largely accepted by acclamation and regularly worshipped in Washington and beyond. As the funding continues to pour in, the NSS has transformed itself into something like a shadow government in that city, while precluding from all serious discussion the possibility of its own future dismantlement or what could replace it. It has made more immediate dangers than terrorism to the health and well-being of Americans seem, at best, secondary. It has pumped fear into the American soul. It is a religion of state power. No Martian could mistake it for anything else.

The Making of a Global Security State

It's become common since 9/11 to speak of a "national security state." But if Edward Snowden's ongoing revelations about NSA surveillance practices have revealed anything, it's that the term is already grossly outdated. Based on what we now know, we should be talking about an American global security state.

Much attention has, understandably enough, been lavished on the phone and other metadata about American citizens that the NSA has been sweeping up and on the ways in which such activities may be abrogating the First and Fourth Amendments of the US Constitution. Far less attention has been paid to the ways in which the NSA (and other US intelligence outfits) are sweeping up global data in part via the Snowden-revealed PRISM and other surveillance programs.

Sometimes naming practices are revealing in themselves, and the NSA's key data-mining tool, capable in March 2013 of gathering "97 billion pieces of intelligence from computer networks worldwide," has been named "Boundless Informant." If you want a sense of where the US Intelligence Community imagines itself going, you couldn't ask for a better hint than that word "boundless." It seems that for our spooks, there are, conceptually speaking, no limits left on this planet.

Today that "community" seeks to put not just the United States but the world fully under its penetrating gaze. By now, the first "heat map" has been published showing where such information is being sucked up on a monthly basis: Iran tops the list (14 billion pieces of intelligence); then come Pakistan (13.5 billion), Jordan (12.7 billion), Egypt (7.6 billion), and India (6.3 billion). Even for a superpower that has unprecedented numbers of military bases scattered across the planet and has divided the world into six military commands, this represents something new. The only question is what?

The twentieth century was the century of "totalitarianisms." We don't yet have a name, a term, for the surveillance structures Washington is building in this century, but there can be no question that, whatever the present constraints on the system, "total" has something to do with it and that we are being ushered into a new world. Despite the recent leaks, we still undoubtedly have a very limited picture of just what the present American surveillance world really looks like and what it plans for our future. One thing is clear, however: the ambitions behind it are staggering and global.

In the classic totalitarian regimes of the previous century, a secret police/surveillance force attempted, via every imaginable method—including informers, wiretappers, torture techniques, imprisonment, and so on—to take total control of a national environment, to turn every citizen's life into the equivalent of an open book, or more accurately a closed, secret file lodged somewhere in that police system. The most impressive of these efforts, the most global, was the Soviet one simply because the Union of Soviet Socialist Republics (USSR) was an imperial power with a set of disparate almost-states—those SSRs of the Caucasus and Central Asia—within its borders and a series of Eastern European satellite states under its control as well. None of the twentieth-century totalitarian regimes, however, ever imagined doing the same thing on a genuinely global scale. There was no way to do so.

Washington's urge to take control of the global communications environment, lock, stock, and chat room—to gather its "data" (billions and billions of pieces of it) and, via inconceivably powerful computer systems, mine and arrange it, find patterns in it, and so turn the world into a secret set of connections—represents a remarkable development. For the first time, a great power wants to know, up close and personal, not just what its own citizens are doing but those of distant lands as well: who they are communicating with, and how, and why, and what they are buying, and where they are traveling, and who they are bumping into (online and over the phone).

Until recently, once you left the environs of science fiction, such a development was simply beyond imagining. You could certainly find precursors for it in, for instance, the Cold War intelligence community's urge to create a global satellite system that would bring every corner of the planet under a new kind of surveillance regime that would map it thoroughly and identify what was being mapped down to the square inch, but nothing so globally up close and personal.

Personal Transparency / Government Opacity

The desire to possess you, or everything that can be known about you, has clearly taken possession of our global security state. With this, it's become increasingly apparent, go other disturbing trends. Take something seemingly unrelated: the recent Supreme Court decision that allows the police to take a DNA swab from an arrestee (if the crime he or she is charged with is "serious"). Theoretically, this is being done for "identification" purposes, but in fact it's being put to other uses entirely, especially in the solving of unconnected crimes.

If you stop to think about it, this development, in turn, represents a remarkable new level of state intrusion on private life, on your self. It means that, for the first time, in a sure-to-widen set of circumstances, the state increasingly has access not just—as with NSA surveillance—to your Internet codes and communications, but to your most basic code of all, your DNA. As Justice Antonin Scalia put it in his dissent in the case, "Make no mistake about it: As an entirely predictable consequence of today's decision, your DNA can be taken and entered into a national DNA database if you are ever arrested, rightly or wrongly, and for whatever reason." Can global DNA databases be far behind?

If your DNA becomes the possession of the state, then you are a transparent human being at the most basic level imaginable. At every level, however, the pattern, the trend, the direction is the same (and it's the same whether you're talking about the government or giant corporations). Increasingly, access to you, your codes, your communications, your purchases, your credit card transactions, your location, your travels, your exchanges with friends, your tastes, your likes and dislikes, is what's wanted—for what's called your "safety" in the case of the government and your business in the case of corporations.

Both want access to everything that can be known about you, because who knows until later what may prove the crucial piece of information to uncover a terrorist network or lure in a new network of customers. They want everything, at least, that can be run through a system of massive computers and sorted into patterns of various potentially useful kinds. You are to be, in this sense, the transparent man or transparent woman.

Your acts, your life patterns, your rights, your codes are to be an open book to them—and increasingly a closed book to you. You are to be their secret and that "you" is an ever more global one. Yet the government, simultaneously, is to become ever less accessible, ever more impenetrable, ever less knowable to you (except in the forms in which government officials would prefer you to know them). None of their codes or secrets are to be accessed by you on pain of imprisonment. Everything in the government—which once was thought to be "your" government—is increasingly disappearing into a professional universe of secrecy. Government officials are classifying tens of millions of documents annually on the same principle that they use in collecting seemingly meaningless or harmless information from you: that only in retrospect can anyone know whether a benign-looking document might prove anything but. Better to deny access to everything.

In the process, they are finding new ways of imposing silence on you, even when it comes to yourself. Since 2001, for instance, it has become possible for the FBI to present you with a National Security Letter, which forces you to turn over information to them, but, far more strikingly, gags you from ever mentioning such a letter. Those who have received them are legally enjoined from discussing or even acknowledging what's happening to them; their lives, in other words, are no longer theirs to discuss. If that isn't Orwellian, what is?

President Barack Obama offered this reassurance in the wake of the Snowden leaks: the NSA, he insisted, is operating under the supervision of all three branches of the government. In fact, the opposite could be said to be true. All three branches, especially in their oversight roles, have been brought within the penumbra of secrecy of the global security state and effectively co-opted or muzzled. This is obviously true with our ex-professor of constitutional law and the executive branch he presides over, which has in recent years been ramping up its own secret operations.

When it comes to Congress, the people's representatives who are to perform oversight on the secret world have been presented with the equivalent of National Security Letters; that is, when let in on some of the secrets of that world, they find they can't discuss them, can't tell the American people about them, can't openly debate them in Congress. We now know that in public sessions with Congress, those who run our most secret outfits, if pushed to the wall by difficult questions, will as a concession respond in the "least untruthful manner" possible, as director of national intelligence James Clapper put it.

Given the secret world's control over Congress, representatives who are horrified by what they've learned about our government's secrecy and surveillance practices, like Democratic senators Ron Wyden and Mark Udall, can only hint at their worries and fears. They can, in essence, wink at you, signal to you in obscure ways that something is out of whack, but they can't tell you directly. Secrecy, after all.

Similarly, the judiciary, that third branch of government and other body of oversight, has, in the twenty-first century, been fully welcomed into the global security state's atmosphere of total secrecy. So when the surveillance crews go to the judiciary for permission to listen in on the world, they go to a secret court, a Foreign Intelligence Surveillance Act (FISA) court, locked within that secret world. It, in turn, notoriously rubber-stamps whatever it is they want to do, evidently offering no resistance whatsoever. (Of the 6,556 electronic surveillance requests submitted to the court in Obama's first term in office, for instance, only one was denied.) In addition, unlike with proceedings in any other court in America, we, the American people, the transparent and ignorant public, can know next to nothing about these. And you know perfectly well why: the overriding needs of secrecy.

The Urge to Expand

As we've known at least since Dana Priest and William Arkin published their stunning series, "Top Secret America," in the *Washington Post* in 2010, the US Intelligence Community has expanded to levels unimaginable even in the Cold War era. It now exists on, as Arkin says, an "industrial scale." And its urge to continue growing, to build yet more structures for surveillance, including a vast $2 billion NSA repository in Bluffdale, Utah, that will be capable of holding an almost unimaginable yottabyte of data, is increasingly written into its DNA.

For this restless, endless expansion of surveillance of every sort and at every level, for the nearly half million or possibly far more private contractors, aka "digital Blackwater," now in the government surveillance business—about 70 percent of the national intelligence budget reportedly goes to the private sector these days—and the nearly five million Americans with security clearances (1.4 million with top security clearances, more than a third of them private contractors), the official explanation is "terrorism." It matters little that terrorism as a phenomenon is one of the lesser dangers Americans face in their daily lives or that, for some of the larger ones, ranging from food-borne illnesses to cars, guns, and what's now called "extreme weather," no one would think about building vast bureaucratic structures shrouded in secrecy, funded to the hilt, and offering Americans promises of ultimate safety.

Terrorism certainly rears its ugly head from time to time, and there's no question that the fear of some operation getting through the US security net drives the employees of our global security state. As an explanation for the phenomenal growth of that state, however, it simply doesn't hold water. In truth, compared to the previous century, US enemies are in remarkably short supply. So forget the official explanation and imagine our security-state-in-the-making in the grips of a kind of compulsive disorder in which the urge to go global, make the most private information of the citizen everywhere the property of the American state, and expand surveillance endlessly simply trumps any other way of doing things.

In other words, they can't help themselves. The process, the phenomenon, has them by the throat, so much so that they can imagine no other way of being. In this mindset, they are paving the way for a new global security—or rather insecurity—world. They are, for instance, hiking spending on "cybersecurity," have already secretly launched the planet's first cyberwar and are planning for more of them, intend to dominate the future cyber-landscape, continue to gather global data on a massive scale, and more generally are acting in ways that they would consider criminal if engaged in by other countries.

TWO

How the US Intelligence Community
Came Out of the Shadows

The 1950s and early 1960s. Weren't those the greatest of days if you were in the American spy game? Governments went down in Guatemala and Iran, thanks to you. In distant Indonesia, Laos, and Vietnam, what a role you played! And even that botch-up of an invasion in Cuba was nothing to sneeze at. In those days, however, you—particularly those of you in the CIA—didn't get the credit you deserved.

You had to live privately with your successes. Sometimes, as with the Bay of Pigs, the failures came back to haunt you (so, in the case of Iran, would your "success," though many years later), but you couldn't with pride talk publicly about what you, in your secret world, had done, or see instant movies and television shows about your triumphs. You couldn't launch a "covert" air war that was reported on, generally positively, almost every week, or bask in the pleasure of having your director claim publicly that it was "the only game in town." You couldn't, that is, come out of what were then called "the shadows" and soak up the glow of attention, be hailed as a hero, join Americans in watching some (fantasy) version of your efforts weekly on television, or get the credit for anything.

Nothing like that was possible—not, at least, until well after two journalists, David Wise and Thomas B. Ross, shined a bright light into those shadows, called you part of an "invisible government," and outed you in ways that you found deeply discomfiting. Their book with that startling title, *The Invisible Government*, was published in 1964 and it was groundbreaking, shadow-removing, illuminating. It caused a fuss from its very first paragraph, which was then a shockeroo: "There are two governments in the United States today. One is visible. The other is invisible." I mean, what did Americans know at the time about an invisible government even the president didn't control, lodged deep inside the government they had elected? Wise and Ross continued: "The first is the government that citizens read about in their newspapers and children study about in their civics books. The second is the interlocking, hidden machinery that carries out the policies of the United States in the Cold War. This second, invisible government gathers intelligence, conducts espionage, and plans and executes secret operations all over the globe."

The Invisible Government came out just as what became known as "the sixties" really began, a moment when lights were suddenly being shined into many previously shadowy American corners. I was then twenty years old, and sometime in those years I read their book with a suitable sense of dread, just as I had read those civics books in high school in which Martians landed on Main Street in some "typical" American town to be amazed by our Constitution.

I wasn't alone reading *The Invisible Government*, either. It was a bestseller, and CIA director John McCone reportedly had read the manuscript, which he had secretly obtained from publisher Random House. He demanded deletions. When the publisher refused, he considered buying up the full first printing. In the end, he evidently tried to arrange for some bad reviews instead.

Time Machines and Shadow Worlds

By 1964, the US Intelligence Community, or IC, had nine members, including the CIA, the Defense Intelligence Agency (DIA), and the National Security Agency (NSA). As Wise and Ross portrayed it, the IC was already a labyrinthine set of secret outfits with growing power. It was capable of launching covert actions worldwide, with a "broad spectrum of domestic operations," the ability to overthrow foreign governments, some involvement in shaping presidential campaigns, and the capacity to plan operations without the knowledge of Congress or full presidential control. "No outsider," they concluded, "can tell whether this activity is necessary or even legal. No outsider is in a position to determine whether or not, in time, these activities might become an internal danger to a free society." Modestly enough, they called for Americans to face the problem and bring "secret power" under control. ("If we err as a society, let it be on the side of control," they wrote.)

Now, imagine that H. G. Wells's time machine had been available in that year of publication. Imagine that it whisked those journalists, then in their mid-thirties, and the young Tom Engelhardt instantly fifty years into the future to survey just how their cautionary tale about a great democratic and republican nation running off the rails had played out.

The first thing they might notice is that the IC of today, with seventeen official outfits, has, by the simplest of calculations, almost doubled. The real size and power of that secret world, however, has in every imaginable way grown staggeringly larger than that. Take one outfit, now part of the IC, that didn't exist back in 1964, the National Geospatial-Intelligence Agency.

The National Geospatial-Intelligence Agency. Photograph by Trevor Paglen. From *The Intercept.*

With an annual budget of close to $5 billion, it recently built a gigantic $1.8 billion headquarters—"the third-largest structure in the Washington area, nearly rivaling the Pentagon in size"—for its sixteen thousand employees. It literally has its "eye" on the globe in a way that would have been left to sci-fi novels almost half a century ago and is tasked as "the nation's primary source of geospatial intelligence, or GEOINT."

Or consider an outfit that did exist then: the National Security Agency, or NSA (once known jokingly as "No Such Agency" because of its deep cover).

The headquarters of the National Security Agency, then and now. The first image, released by the NSA, is believed to be from the 1970s. The second image, from 2003, is from photographer Trevor Paglen. From *The Intercept.*

Like its geospatial cousin, it has been in a period of explosive growth, budgetary and otherwise, capped by the construction of that "heavily fortified" data center in Utah. According to NSA expert James Bamford, the center was built to "intercept, decipher, analyze, and store vast swaths of the world's communications as they zap down from satellites and zip through the underground and undersea cables of international, foreign, and domestic networks." He adds: "Flowing through its servers and routers and stored in near-bottomless databases will be all forms of communication, including the complete contents of private emails, cell phone calls, and Google searches, as well as all sorts of personal data trails—parking receipts, travel itineraries, bookstore purchases, and other digital 'pocket litter.'" We're talking not just about foreign terrorists here but about the intake and eternal storage of vast reams of material from American citizens, possibly even you.

Or consider a little-known post-9/11 creation, the National Counterterrorism Center (NCTC), which is not even a separate agency in the IC but part of the Office of the Director of National Intelligence. According to the *Wall Street Journal*, the Obama administration has turned that organization into "a government dragnet, sweeping up millions of records about US citizens—even people suspected of no crime." It has granted the NCTC the right, among other things,

> to examine the government files of US citizens for possible criminal behavior, even if there is no reason to suspect them . . . copy entire government databases—flight records, casino-employee lists, the names of Americans hosting foreign-exchange students, and many others. The agency has new authority to keep data about innocent US citizens for up to five years, and to analyze it for suspicious patterns of behavior. Previously, both were prohibited.

Or take the Defense Intelligence Agency, which came into existence in 1961 and became operational only the year *The Invisible Government* was published. Almost half a century ago, as Wise and Ross told their readers, it had 2,500 employees and a relatively modest set of assigned tasks. By the end of the Cold War, it had 7,500 employees. Two decades later, another tale of explosive growth: the DIA now has 16,500 employees.

And then there's the National Reconnaissance Office (NRO). Max Ehrenfreund, reporting on "a top-secret budget document that former

The National Reconnaissance Office. Photography by Trevor Paglen.
From *The Intercept.*

NSA contractor Edward Snowden provided to *The Washington Post*,"
found that the NRO, which "operates satellites and other remote sensors,"
has a budget of $10.3 billion a year, behind only the CIA and NSA, and
up 12 percent from 2004.

In their 2010 "Top Secret America" series, Dana Priest and William
Arkin caught a spirit of untrammeled expansion in the post-9/11 era that
would surely have amazed those two authors who had called for "controls" over the secret world: "In Washington and the surrounding area,
33 building complexes for top-secret intelligence work are under construction or have been built since September 2001. Together they occupy
the equivalent of almost three Pentagons or 22 U.S. Capitol buildings—
about 17 million square feet of space."

Similarly, the combined IC budget, which in deepest secrecy had
supposedly soared to at least $44 billion in 2005 (all such figures have to
be taken with a dumpster-ful of salt), has by now reached an official $67.6
billion, even after sequester cuts.

Let's add in one more futuristic shocker for our time travelers. Someone would have to tell them that, in 1991, the Soviet Union, that great

imperial power and nemesis of the invisible government, with its vast army, secret police, system of gulags, and monstrous nuclear arsenal, had disappeared largely nonviolently from the face of the earth, and no single power has since arisen to challenge the United States militarily. In other words, that ballooning US intelligence budget, the explosion of new construction, the steep growth in personnel, and all the rest have happened in a world in which the United States is facing a couple of rickety regional powers (Iran and North Korea), a minority insurgency in Afghanistan, a rising economic power (China) with still modest military might, and probably a few thousand extreme Muslim fundamentalists and al-Qaeda wannabes scattered around the planet.

They would have to be told that, thanks to a single horrific event, a kind of terrorist luck-out we now refer to in shorthand as "9/11," and despite the diminution of global enemies, an already enormous IC has expanded nonstop in a country seized by a spasm of fear and paranoia.

Preparing Battlefields and Building Giant Embassies

Dumbfounded by the size of the invisible government they had once anatomized, the two reporters might have been no less surprised by another development: the way in our own time "intelligence" has been militarized while the US military itself has plunged into the shadows. Of course, it's now well-known that the CIA, a civilian intelligence agency headed for a while by a retired four-star general, has been paramilitarized and is now putting a significant part of its energy into running an ever spreading "covert" set of drone wars across the Greater Middle East.

Meanwhile, since the early years of the George W. Bush administration, the US military has been intent on claiming some of the CIA's turf as its own. Not long after the 9/11 attacks, then secretary of defense Donald Rumsfeld began pushing the Pentagon into CIA-style intelligence activities—the "full spectrum of humint [human intelligence] operations"—to "prepare" for future "battlefields." That process has never ended. In April 2012, for instance, the Pentagon released the information that it was in the process of setting up a new spy agency called the Defense Clandestine Service (DCS). Its job: to globalize military "intelligence" by taking it beyond the obvious war zones. The DCS was tasked as well with working more closely with the CIA (while assumedly rivaling it).

As Greg Miller of the *Washington Post* reported, "Creation of the new service also coincides with the appointment of a number of senior officials at the Pentagon who have extensive backgrounds in intelligence and firm opinions on where the military's spying programs—often seen as lackluster by CIA insiders—have gone wrong."

And then, in December 2012, the head of the DIA, originally a place for analysis and coordination, announced at a conference that his agency was going to expand into "humint" in a big way, filling embassies around the world with a new corps of clandestine operators who had diplomatic or other "cover." He was talking about fielding 1,600 "collectors" who would be "trained by the CIA and often work with the Joint Special Operations Command." Never, in other words, will a country have had so many "diplomats" who know absolutely nothing about diplomacy.

Though the Senate balked at funding the expansion of the DCS, all of this represents both a significant reshuffling of what is still called "intelligence" but is really a form of low-level war-making on a global stage and a continuing expansion of America's secret world on a scale hitherto unimaginable—all in the name, of course, of "national security." Now at least, it's easier to understand why, from London to Baghdad to Islamabad, the United States has been building humongous embassies, fortified like ancient castles and the size of imperial palaces, for unparalleled staffs of "diplomats." These will now clearly include scads of CIA, DIA, and perhaps DCS agents, among others, under diplomatic cover.

Into this mix should go another outfit unknown to Wise and Ross, but one—given the publicity SEAL Team 6 has gotten over the raid that killed Osama bin Laden and other activities—of which most Americans will be at least somewhat aware. An ever-greater role in the secret world is now being played by a military organization that long ago headed into the shadows, the Joint Special Operations Command (JSOC). In 2009, *New Yorker* reporter Seymour Hersh termed it an "executive assassination ring" (especially in Iraq) that did not "report to anybody, except in the Bush-Cheney days . . . directly to the Cheney office."

In fact, JSOC only emerged into the public eye when one of its key operatives in Iraq, General Stanley McChrystal, was appointed US war commander in Afghanistan. It has been in the spotlight ever since as it engages in what once might have been CIA-style paramilitary operations on steroids, increases its intelligence-gathering capacity, runs its own drone wars, and has set up a new headquarters in Washington, fifteen convenient minutes from the White House.

Big-Screen Moments and "Covert" Wars

At their top levels, the leaderships of the CIA, the DIA, and JSOC are now mixing and matching in a blur of ever more intertwined, militarized outfits, always on a perpetual war footing. They have, in this way, turned the ancient arts of intelligence, surveillance, spying, and assassination into a massively funded way of life and are now regularly conducting war on the sly and on the loose across the globe.

This shadow government now represents an irreversible way of life, one that is increasingly celebrated in this country. It is also part of the seemingly endless growth of the imperial power of the White House, and, in ways that Wise and Ross would in 1964 have found inconceivable, is beyond all accountability or control when it comes to the American people.

It is also ready to take public credit for its "successes" (or even a significant hand in shaping how they are viewed in the public arena). Once upon a time, a CIA agent who died in some covert operation would have gone unnamed and unacknowledged. By the 1970s, that agent would have had a star engraved on the wall of the lobby of CIA headquarters, but no one outside the Agency would have known about his or her fate. Now, those who die in our "secret" operations or ones launched against our "invisible" agents can become public figures and celebrated "heroes." This was the case, for instance, with Jennifer Matthews, a CIA agent who died in Afghanistan when an Agency double agent turned out to be a triple agent and suicide bomber. Or when a soldier from SEAL Team 6 died in a raid in Afghanistan to rescue a kidnapped doctor. The navy released his photo and name, and he was widely hailed. This would certainly have been striking to Wise and Ross.

Then again, they would undoubtedly have been no less startled to discover that, from Jack Ryan and Jason Bourne to *Syriana*, the *Mission Impossible* films, and *Taken*, the CIA and other secret outfits (or their fantasy doppelgangers) have become staples of American multiplexes. Nor has the small screen, from *24* to *Homeland*, been immune to this invasion of visibility. Or consider this: just over a year and a half after SEAL Team 6's super-secret bin Laden operation ended, it had already been turned into *Zero Dark Thirty*, a highly praised (and controversial) movie with a heroine patterned on an undercover CIA agent whose photo made it into the public arena. Moreover, it was a film whose makers were reportedly aided or at least encouraged in their efforts by the CIA, the Pentagon, and the White House, just as the SEALs aided the high-grossing movie *Act of Valor* ("an elite team of Navy SEALs . . . embark on a covert mission to recover a kidnapped CIA agent") by lending the film actual SEALs as (unnamed) actors and then staging a SEAL parachute drop onto a red carpet at its Hollywood premiere.

True, at the time *The Invisible Government* was published, the first two James Bond films were already hits and the *Mission Impossible* TV show was only two years from launch, but the way the invisible world has since emerged from the shadows to become a fixture of pop culture remains stunning. And don't think this was just some cultural quirk. After all, back in the 1960s, enterprising reporters had to pry open those invisible agencies to discover anything about what they were doing. In those years, for instance, the CIA ran a secret air and ground war in Laos that it tried desperately never to acknowledge despite their formidable size and scope.

Today, on the other hand, the Agency runs what are called "covert" drone wars in Pakistan, Yemen, and Somalia in which most strikes are promptly reported in the press, and about which the administration clearly leaked information to the *New York Times* on the president's role in picking those to die. In the past, American presidents pursued "plausible deniability" when it came to assassination plots like those against Congolese leader Patrice Lumumba, Cuba's Fidel Castro, and Vietnam's Ngo Dinh Diem. Now, assassination is clearly considered a semipublic part of the presidential job, codified, bureaucratized, and regulated (though only within the White House), and remarkably public.

Ever since president Ronald Reagan's CIA-run Central American Contra wars of the 1980s, the definition of "covert" has changed. It no longer means hidden from sight, but beyond accountability. It is now a polite way of saying to the American people: You can feel free to praise it, but you have nothing to do with it, no say over it.

THREE

How to Be a Rogue Superpower

It's hard even to know how to take it in. An employee of a private contractor working for the NSA makes off with unknown numbers of files about America's developing global security state on a thumb drive and four laptop computers, and jumps the nearest plane to Hong Kong. His goal: to expose a vast surveillance structure built in the shadows in the post-9/11 years and significantly aimed at Americans. He leaks some of the documents to the filmmaker Laura Poitras, the journalist Glenn Greenwald, and to the *Washington Post*. The response is unprecedented: an "international manhunt" (or more politely but less accurately, "a diplomatic full court press") conducted not by Interpol or the United Nations but by the planet's sole superpower, the very government whose practices the leaker was so intent on exposing.

And that's just for starters. Let's add another factor. The leaker, a young man with great techno-savvy, lets the world know that he's picked and chosen among the NSA files in his possession. He's releasing only those he thinks the American public needs to know about in order to start a full-scale debate about the unprecedented secret world of surveillance that their taxpayer dollars have created. In other words, this is no "document dump." He wants to spark change without doing harm.

But here's the kicker: he couldn't be more aware of previous whistle-blower cases, the punitive reaction of his government to them, and the fate that might be his. As a result, we now know, he has encrypted the full set of files in his possession and left them in one or more safe places for unknown individuals—that is, we don't know who they are—to access, should he be taken by the United States.

In other words, from the time Edward Snowden's first leaked documents came out, it was obvious that he was in control of how much of the NSA's secret world would be seen. It would be hard then not to conclude that capturing him, imprisoning him, trying him, and throwing away the key is likely to increase, not decrease, the flow of those documents. Knowing that, the Obama administration and the representatives of our secret world went after him anyway—after one man on a global scale and in a way that may not have a precedent. No thought of future embarrassment stopped them, nor, it seems, did they hesitate because of possible resentments engendered by their heavy-handed pressure on numerous foreign governments.

The result has been a global spectacle as well as a worldwide debate about the spying practices of the United States and its allies. Since the revelations became public, Washington has proven determined, vengeful, and implacable. It has strong-armed, threatened, and elbowed powers large and small. It has essentially pledged that Snowden will never be safe on this planet in his lifetime. And yet, to mention the obvious, the greatest power on earth has, thus far, failed to get its man and is losing the public opinion battle globally.

An Asylum-less World

Highlighted in all this has been a curious fact of our twenty-first-century world. In the Cold War years, asylum was always potentially available. If you opposed one of the two superpowers or its allies, the other was usually ready to open its arms to you, as the United States famously did for what were once called "Soviet dissidents" in great numbers. The Soviets did the same for Americans, Brits, and others, often secret Communists, sometimes actual spies, who opposed the leading capitalist power and its global order.

Today, if you are a twenty-first-century "dissident" and need asylum or protection from the only superpower left, there is essentially none to be had. The greatest power on the planet has, since 9/11, shown itself perfectly willing to do almost anything in pursuit of its definition of "security" or the security of its security system. Torture, abuse, the setting up of secret prisons or "black sites," the kidnapping of terrorist suspects (including perfectly innocent people) off the streets of global cities as well as in the backlands of the planet, their "rendition" to the torture chambers of complicit allied regimes, and the secret surveillance of anyone anywhere would only be the start of a far longer list.

If Edward Snowden is proving one thing, it's this: in 2013, Planet Earth isn't big enough to protect the American version of "dissidents." Instead, it looks ever more like a giant prison with a single policeman, judge, jury, and jailer.

The War on Whistleblowers

In the Obama years, the sole superpower has put special effort into deterring anyone in its labyrinthine bureaucracy who shows a desire to let us know what "our" government is doing in our name. The administration's efforts to stop whistleblowers have become legendary. It has even launched an unprecedented program to specially train millions of employees and contractors to profile coworkers for "indicators of insider threat behavior." They are being encouraged to inform on any "high-risk persons" they suspect might be planning to go public. Administration officials have also put much punitive energy into making examples out of whistleblowers who have tried to reveal anything of the inner workings of the national security complex.

In this way, the Obama administration has more than doubled the total whistleblower prosecutions of all previous administrations combined under the draconian World War I–era Espionage Act. In addition, it has threatened journalists who have written about or published leaked material and has gone on expeditions into the telephone and email records of major media organizations.

All this adds up to a new version of deterrence thinking in which a potential whistleblower should know that he or she will experience a lifetime of suffering for leaking anything; in which those, even in the highest reaches of government, who consider speaking to journalists on classified subjects should know that their calls could be monitored and their whispers criminalized; and in which the media should know that reporting on such subjects is not a healthy activity.

How to Ground a Plane to (Not) Catch a Whistleblower

In this light, no incident has been more revealing than the grounding of the plane of Bolivian president Evo Morales, the democratically elected head of a sovereign Latin American nation that is not an official enemy of the United States. Angry Bolivian authorities termed it a "kidnapping" or "imperialist hijack." It was, at the least, an act for which it's hard to imagine a precedent.

Evidently officials in Washington believed that the plane bringing the Bolivian president back from Moscow was also carrying Snowden. As a result, the United States seems to have put enough pressure on four European countries (France, Spain, Portugal, and Italy) to force that plane to land for refueling in a fifth country (Austria). There—again, US pressure seems to have been the crucial factor—it was searched under disputed circumstances and Snowden not found.

So much is not known about what happened, in part because there was no serious reporting from Washington on the subject. The US media largely ignored the American role in the grounding of the plane, an incident that was regularly described here as if the obvious hadn't happened. This may, at least in part, have been one result of the Obama administration's implacable pursuit of whistleblowers and leakers right into the phone records of reporters. The government has made such a point of its willingness to pursue whistleblowers via journalists that, as Associated Press president Gary Pruitt pointed out, national security sources are drying up. Key figures in Washington are scared to talk even off the record (now that "off" turns out to be potentially very "on"). And the new "tighter" guidelines the Justice Department announced (after much criticism) for accessing reporters' records are clearly filled with loopholes and are undoubtedly little more than window dressing.

Still, it's reasonable to imagine that, when Morales's plane took off from Moscow, there were top US officials gathered in a situation room (à la the bin Laden raid), that the president was in the loop, and that the intelligence people said something like: *We have an 85 percent certainty that Snowden is on that plane.* Obviously, the decision was made to bring it down and enough pressure was placed on key officials in those five countries to cause them to bow to Washington's will.

Imagine for a moment that an American president's plane had been brought down in a similar fashion. Imagine that a consortium of nations pressured by, say, China or Russia did it and that, with the president aboard, it was then searched for a Chinese or Soviet "dissident." Imagine the reaction here, the shock, the accusations of "illegality," of "skyjacking," of "international terrorism." Imagine the 24/7 media coverage and the information pouring out of Washington about what would no doubt have been termed "an act of war."

Of course, such a scenario is inconceivable on this one-way planet. So instead, just think about the silence here over the Morales incident, the lack of coverage, the lack of reporting, the lack of outrage, the lack of shock, the lack of . . .well, just about anything at all.

Slouching toward Washington to Be Born

And yet don't think that no one has been affected, no one intimidated. Consider, for instance, a superior piece of reporting by Eric Lichtblau of the *New York Times*. His July 6, 2013, front-page story, "In Secret, Court Vastly Broadens Powers of NSA," might once have sent shock waves through Washington and perhaps the country as well. It did, after all, reveal how, in "more than a dozen classified rulings," a secret FISA court, which oversees the American surveillance state, "has created a secret body of law," giving the NSA sweeping new powers.

Here's the paragraph that should have had Americans jumping out of their skins:

> The 11-member Foreign Intelligence Surveillance Court, known as the FISA court, was once mostly focused on approving case-by-case wiretapping orders. But since major changes in legislation and greater judicial oversight of intelligence operations were instituted six years ago, it has

quietly become almost a parallel Supreme Court, serving as the ultimate arbiter on surveillance issues and delivering opinions that will most likely shape intelligence practices for years to come, the officials said.

At most moments in American history, the revelation that a secret court that never turns down government requests is making law "almost" at the level of the Supreme Court would surely have caused an outcry in Congress and elsewhere. However, there was none, a sign either of how powerful and intimidating the secret world has become or of how much Congress and the rest of Washington have already been absorbed into it. No less significant—and again, we know so little that it's necessary to read between the lines—Lichtblau indicated that more than six "current and former national security officials," perhaps disturbed by the expanding powers of the FISA court, discussed its classified rulings "on the condition of anonymity." Fittingly enough, Lichtblau wrote a remarkably anonymous piece. Given that sources no longer have any assurance that phone and email records aren't being or won't be monitored, we have no idea how these shadowy figures got in touch with him or vice versa. All we know is that, even when shining a powerful light into the darkness of the surveillance universe, American journalism now finds itself plunging into the shadows as well.

A shadow government, placing its trust in secret courts and the large-scale surveillance of populations, its own included, while pursuing its secret desires globally, was just the sort of thing that the country's founding fathers feared. In the end, it hardly matters under what label—including American "safety" and "security"—such a governing power is built. Sooner or later, the architecture will determine the acts, and it will become more tyrannical at home and more extreme abroad.

It's eerie that some aspects of the totalitarian governments that went down for the count in the twentieth century are now being recreated in those shadows. There, an increasingly "totalistic" if not yet totalitarian beast, its hour come round at last, is slouching toward Washington to be born, while those who cared to shine a little light on the birth process are in jail or being hounded across this planet.

The Powers of the Lockdown State

In the Bush and Obama years, the United States has become a nation not of laws but of legal memos, not of legality but of legalisms—and you don't have to be a lawyer to know it. The result? Secret armies, secret wars, secret surveillance, and spreading state secrecy, which has in turn meant a government of the bureaucrats about which the American people could know next to nothing. And it's all "legal."

Consider, for instance, this passage from a January 2013 *Washington Post* piece on the codification of "targeted killing operations"—in other words, drone assassinations—in what's now called the White House "playbook": "Among the subjects covered . . . are the process for adding names to kill lists, the legal principles that govern when U.S. citizens can be targeted overseas, and the sequence of approvals required when the CIA or U.S. military conducts drone strikes outside war zones."

Those "legal principles" were, of course, being written up by lawyers working for people like then Obama counterterrorism "tsar" John O. Brennan; that is, officials who wanted the greatest possible latitude when it came to knocking off "terrorist suspects," American or otherwise. Imagine, for instance, lawyers hired by a group of neighborhood thieves creating a "playbook" outlining which kinds of houses they considered it legal to break into and just why that might be so. Would the "principles" in that document be written up in the press as "legal" ones?

Here's the kicker. According to the *Post*, the "legal principles" a White House with no intention of limiting (let alone shutting down) America's drone wars had painstakingly established as "law" were not going to be applied to Pakistan's tribal borderlands where the most intense drone strikes were taking place. The CIA's secret drone war there was instead going to be given a free pass for at least a year or more to blast away as it pleased—the White House equivalent of Monopoly's get-out-of-jail-free card.

In other words, even by the White House's definition of legality, what the CIA is doing in Pakistan should be considered illegal. But these days when it comes to anything connected to American war-making, legality is whatever the White House says it is (and you won't find its legalisms seriously challenged by American courts).

The drone strikes, after all, are perfectly "legal." How do we know? Because the administration assures us that it's so, even if they don't care to fully reveal their reasoning, and because, truth be told, on such matters they can do whatever they want. It's legal because they've increasingly become the ones who define legality.

It would, of course, be illegal for Canadians, Pakistanis, or Iranians to fly missile-armed drones over Minneapolis or New York, no less take out their versions of bad guys in the process. That would, among other things, be a breach of American sovereignty. The United States, however, can do more or less what it wants when and where it wants. The reason: it has established, to the satisfaction of our national security managers— and they have the secret legal documents (written by themselves) to prove it—that US drones can cross national boundaries just about anywhere if the bad guys are, in their opinion, bad enough.

As with our distant wars, most Americans are remarkably unaffected in any direct way by the lockdown of this country. And yet in a post-legal drone world of perpetual "wartime," in which fantasies of disaster out-race far more realistic dangers and fears, sooner or later the bin Laden tax will take its toll, the chickens will come home to roost, and they will be able to do anything in our name (without even worrying about producing secret legal memos to justify their acts). By then, we'll be completely locked down and the key thrown away.

The Enemy-Industrial Complex

All these years, while we've been launching wars and pursuing a "global war on terror," we've poured money into national security as if there were no tomorrow. From our police to our borders, we've up-armored everywhere. We constantly hear about "threats" to us and to the "homeland." And yet, when you knock on the door marked "Enemy," there's seldom anyone home. The original al-Qaeda is largely decimated, al-Qaeda in the Arabian Peninsula is located in the poorest areas of poverty-stricken Yemen, the Taliban is in poverty-stricken Afghanistan, unnamed jihadis are scattered across poverty-stricken areas of North Africa, and Iran is a relatively weak regional power run by not particularly adept theocrats. Few in this country have found this worth contemplating. Few seem to notice any disjuncture between the enemy-ridden, threatening, and deeply dangerous world we have spent the last decade-plus preparing ourselves for (and fighting in) and the world as it actually is—even those who lived through significant parts of the last, anxiety-producing, bloody century.

The United States, in other words, is probably in less danger from external enemies than at any moment in the last century. There is no other imperial power on the planet capable of, or desirous of, taking on American power directly, including China. It's true that, on September 11, 2001, nineteen hijackers with box cutters produced a remarkable, apocalyptic, and devastating TV show in which almost three thousand people died. When those giant towers in downtown New York collapsed, it certainly had the look of nuclear disaster (and in those first days, the media was filled with nuclear-style references), but it wasn't actually an apocalyptic event. The enemy was still nearly nonexistent. The act cost bin Laden only an estimated $400,000 to $500,000, though it would lead to a series of trillion-dollar wars. It was a nightmarish event that had a malign *Wizard of Oz* quality to it: a tiny man producing giant effects. It in no way endangered the state. In fact, it would actually strengthen many of its powers. It put a hit on the economy, but a passing one. It was a spectacular and spectacularly gruesome act of terror by a small, murderous organization then capable of mounting a major operation somewhere on earth only once every couple of years. It was meant to spread fear but nothing more.

When the towers came down and you could suddenly see to the horizon, it was still, in historical terms, remarkably unthreatening. And yet 9/11 was experienced here as a Pearl Harbor moment—a sneak attack by a terrifying enemy meant to disable the country. The next day, newspaper headlines were filled with variations on "A Pearl Harbor of the Twenty-First Century." If it was a repeat of December 7, 1941, however, it lacked an imperial Japan or any other state to declare war on, although one of the weakest partial states on the planet, the Taliban's Afghanistan, would end up filling the bill adequately enough for Americans.

To put this in perspective, consider two obvious major dangers in US life: suicide by gun and death by car. In 2010, more than 19,000 Americans killed themselves using guns. (In the same year, there were "only" 11,000 homicides nationwide.) In 2011, 32,000 Americans died in traffic accidents. In other words, Americans accept without blinking the equivalent yearly of more than six 9/11s in suicides-by-gun and more than ten when it comes to vehicular deaths. Similarly, had the so-called underwear bomber, to take one post-9/11 example of terrorism, succeeded in downing Flight 253 and murdering its 290 passengers, it would indeed have been a horrific act of terror, but he and his compatriots would have had to bring down 65 planes to reach the annual level of weaponized suicides and more than 110 planes when it comes to vehicular deaths.

And yet no one has declared war on either the car or the gun (or the companies that make them or the people who sell them). No one has built a massive, nearly trillion-dollar car-and-gun-security-complex to deal with them. In the case of guns, quite the opposite is true, as the debate over gun control after the Sandy Hook Elementary School shooting in Newtown, Connecticut, in December 2012 made all too clear. On both scores, Americans have decided to live with perfectly real dangers and the staggering carnage that accompanies them, constraining them on occasion or sometimes not at all.

Despite the carnage of 9/11, terrorism has been a small-scale American danger in the years since, worse than shark attacks but not much else. Like a wizard, however, what Osama bin Laden and his suicide bombers did that day was create an instant sense of an enemy so big and so powerful that Americans found "war" a reasonable response: big enough for those who wanted an international police action against al-Qaeda to be laughed out of the room; big enough to launch an invasion of revenge against Iraq, a country unrelated to al-Qaeda; big enough, in fact, to essentially declare war on the world. It took next to no time for top administration officials to begin talking about targeting sixty countries, and as journalist Ron Suskind has reported, within six days of the attack, the CIA had topped that figure, presenting President Bush with a "Worldwide Attack Matrix," a plan that targeted terrorists in eighty countries.

What's remarkable is how little noted was the disjuncture between the scope and scale of the global war that was almost instantly launched and the actual enemy. You could certainly make a reasonable argument that, in these years, Washington has largely fought no one—and lost. Everywhere it went it created enemies who had previously hardly existed, and the process is ongoing. Had you been able to time-travel back to the Cold War era to inform Americans that, in the future, our major enemies would be in Afghanistan, Yemen, Somalia, Mali, Libya, and so on, they would surely have thought you mad.

Without a sufficiently threatening enemy, so much that has been done in Washington in these years would have been unattainable. The vast national security building and spending spree would have been unlikely.

Without the fear of an enemy capable of doing almost anything, money at ever escalating levels would never have poured into homeland security, or the Pentagon, or a growing complex of crony corporations associated with our weaponized safety. The exponential growth of the national security complex, as well as of the powers of the executive branch when it comes to national security matters, would have been inconceivable.

Without 9/11 and the perpetual "wartime" that has followed, along with the heavily promoted threat of terrorists ready to strike and potentially capable of wielding biological, chemical, or even nuclear weapons, we would have no Department of Homeland Security or the lucrative mini-homeland-security complex that surrounds it; our endless drone wars and the "drone lobby" that goes with them might never have developed; and the US military would not have an ever growing secret military, the Joint Special Operations Command (JSOC), gestating inside it—effectively the president's private army, air force, and navy—conducting largely secret operations across much of the planet.

For all of this to happen, there had to be an enemy-industrial complex—a network of crucial figures and institutions ready to pump up the threat we faced and convince Americans that we were in a world so dangerous that rights, liberty, and privacy were small things to sacrifice for American safety. In short, any number of interests ranging from Bush administration officials eager to "sweep it all up" and do whatever they wanted to weapons makers, lobbyists, surveillance outfits, think tanks, military intellectuals, and assorted pundits...well, the whole national and homeland security racket and its various hangers-on had an interest in beefing up the enemy. For them, it was important in the post-9/11 era that threats would never again lack a capital "T" or a hefty dollar sign.

Post-9/11, major media outlets were generally prepared to take the enemy-industrial complex's word for it and play every new terrorist incident as if it were potentially the end of the world. Increasingly as the years went on, jobs, livelihoods, and an expanding world of "security" depended on the continuance of all this; depended, in short, on the injection of regular doses of fear into the body politic.

That was the "favor" Osama bin Laden did for Washington's national security apparatus and the Bush administration on that fateful September morning. He engraved a belief in the American brain that would live on indelibly for years, possibly decades, calling for eternal vigilance at any cost and on a previously unknown scale. As the Project for the New American Century (PNAC), that neocon think-tank-cum-government-in-waiting, so fatefully put it in "Rebuilding America's Defenses" a year before the 9/11 attacks: "Further, the process of transformation [of the military], even if it brings revolutionary change, is likely to be a long one, absent some catastrophic and catalyzing event—like a new Pearl Harbor." So when the new Pearl Harbor arrived out of the blue, with many PNAC members (from vice president Dick Cheney on down) already in office, they naturally saw their chance. They created an al-Qaeda on steroids and launched their "global war" to establish a Pax Americana in the Middle East and then perhaps globally. They were aware that they lacked opponents of the stature of those of the previous century and, in their documents, they made it clear that they were planning to ensure no future great-power-style enemy or bloc of enemy-like nations would arise. Ever.

For this, they needed an American public anxious, frightened, and ready to pay. It was, in other words, in their interest to manipulate us. And if that were all there was to it, our world would be a grim but simple enough place. As it happens, it's not. Ruling elites, no matter what power they have, don't work that way. Before they manipulate us, they almost invariably manipulate themselves.

I was convinced of this years ago by Jim Peck, a friend who had spent a lot of time reading early Cold War documents from the National Security Council—from, that is, a small group of powerful governmental figures writing to and for each other in the utmost secrecy. As he told me then and wrote in *Washington's China*, an insightful book on the early US response to the establishment of the People's Republic of China, what struck him in the documents was the crudely anticommunist language those men used in private with each other. It was the sort of anticommunism you might otherwise have assumed Washington's ruling elite would only have wielded to manipulate ordinary Americans with fears of Communist subversion, the "enemy within," and Soviet plans to take over the world. They were indeed manipulative men, but before they influenced other Americans they appeared to have undergone something like a process of collective autohypnotism in which they convinced one another of the dangers they needed the American people to believe in.

There is evidence that a similar process took place in the aftermath of 9/11. From the flustered look on George W. Bush's face as his plane took him not toward but away from Washington on September 11, 2001, to the image of Dick Cheney being chauffeured around Washington in an armored motorcade with a "gas mask and a biochemical survival suit" in the backseat, you could sense that the enemy loomed large and omnipresent for them. They were, that is, genuinely scared, even if they were also ready to make use of that fear for their own ends.

Or consider the issue of Saddam Hussein's supposed weapons of mass destruction (WMD), that excuse for the invasion of Iraq. Critics of the invasion are generally quick to point out how that bogus issue was used by the top officials of the Bush administration to gain public support for a course that they had already chosen. After all, Cheney and his men cherry-picked the evidence to make their case, even formed their own secret intel outfit to give them what they needed. In the process, they ignored facts at hand that brought their version of events into question. They publicly claimed in an orchestrated way that Saddam had active nuclear and WMD programs. They spoke in the most open fashion of potential mushroom clouds from (nonexistent) Iraqi nuclear weapons rising over American cities, or of those same cities being sprayed with (nonexistent) chemical or biological weapons from (nonexistent) Iraqi drones. They certainly had to know that some of this information was useful but bogus. Still, they had clearly also convinced themselves that, on taking Iraq, they would indeed find some Iraqi WMD to justify their claims.

In his book *Dirty Wars*, the journalist Jeremy Scahill cites the conservative reporter Rowan Scarborough on then secretary of defense Donald Rumsfeld's growing post-invasion irritation over the search for Iraqi

WMD sites. "Each morning," wrote Scarborough, "the crisis action team had to report that another location was a bust. Rumsfeld grew angrier and angrier. One officer quoted him as saying, 'They must be there!' At one briefing, he picked up the briefing slides and tossed them back at the briefers." In other words, those top officials hustling us into their global war and their long-desired invasion of Iraq had also hustled themselves into the same world with a similar set of fears. This may seem odd, but given the workings of the human mind, its ability to comfortably hold potentially contradictory thoughts most of the time without disturbing itself greatly, it's not.

A similar phenomenon undoubtedly took place in the larger national security establishment, where self-interest combined easily enough with fear. After all, in the post-9/11 era, they were promising us one thing: something close to 100 percent "safety" when it came to one small danger in our world—terrorism. The fear that the next underwear bomber might get through surely had not only the American public but also the American security state in its grips. After all, who loses the most if another shoe bomber strikes, another ambassador goes down, another 9/11 actually happens? Whose job, whose world, will be at stake then?

They may indeed have been a crew of Machiavellis, but they were also acolytes in the cult of terror and global war. They lived in the Cathedral of the Enemy. They were the first believers and they will undoubtedly be the last ones as well. They were invested in the importance of the enemy. It was, and remains, their religion. They are, after all, the enemy-industrial complex and if we are in its grip, so are they.

The comic strip character Pogo once famously declared: "We have met the enemy and he is us." How true. We just don't know it yet.

FOUR

Mistaking Omniscience for Omnipotence

Given how similar they sound and how logical it is to imagine one leading to the other, confusing omniscience (total knowledge) with omnipotence (total power) is easy enough. It's a reasonable supposition that, before the Edward Snowden revelations hit, America's spymasters had made just that mistake. If the drip-drip-drip of Snowden's mother of all leaks has taught us anything, however, it should be this: omniscience is not omnipotence. At least on the global political scene today, they may bear remarkably little relation to each other. In fact, at the moment, Washington seems to be operating in a world in which the more you know about the secret lives of others, the less powerful you turn out to be.

The slow-tease pulling back of the NSA curtain to reveal the skeletal surveillance structure embedded in our planet (what cheekbones!) has been an epochal event. It's visibly changed attitudes around the world toward the US government—strikingly for the worse, even if this hasn't fully sunk in here yet. Domestically, the inability to put the issue to sleep or tuck it away somewhere has left the Obama administration, Congress, and the Intelligence Community increasingly at one another's throats. And somewhere in a system made for leaks, there are young techies inside a surveillance machine so viscerally appalling, so like the worst sci-fi scenarios they read while growing up, that—no matter the penalties—one of them, two of them, many of them are likely to become the next Edward Snowden(s).

Conceptually speaking, we've never seen anything like the NSA's urge to eavesdrop on, spy on, monitor, record, and save every communication of any sort on the planet—to keep track of humanity, all of humanity, from its major leaders to obscure figures in the backlands of the globe. And the fact is that, within the scope of what might be technologically feasible in our era, they seem not to have missed an opportunity.

The NSA is everywhere, gobbling up emails, phone calls, texts, tweets, Facebook posts, credit card sales, communications and transactions of every conceivable sort. The NSA and British intelligence are feeding off the fiber optic cables that carry Internet and phone activity. The agency stores records ("metadata") of every phone call made in the United States. In various ways, legal and otherwise, its operatives long ago slipped through the conveniently ajar back doors of media giants like Yahoo, Verizon, and Google—and also in conjunction with British intelligence they have been secretly collecting records from the private networks of Yahoo and Google to the tune of 181 million communications in a single month, or more than two billion a year.

Meanwhile, their privately hired corporate hackers have systems that, among other things, can slip inside your computer to count and view every keystroke you make. Thanks to that mobile phone of yours (even when it's off), those same hackers can locate you just about anywhere on the planet. And that's just to begin to summarize what we know of their still developing global surveillance state.

In other words, there's my email and your phone metadata, and his tweets and her texts, and the swept-up records of billions of cell phone calls and other communications by French and Nigerians, Italians and Pakistanis, Germans and Yemenis, Egyptians and Spaniards, and don't forget the Chinese, Vietnamese, Indonesians, and Burmese, among others, and it would be a reasonable bet to include just about any other nationality you care to mention. Then there are the NSA listening posts at all those US embassies and consulates around the world, and the reports on the way the agency listened in on the United Nations, bugged European Union offices "on both sides of the Atlantic," accessed computers inside the Indian embassy in Washington, DC, and that country's UN mission in New York, hacked into the computer network of and spied on Brazil's largest oil company, Petrobras (Petróleo Brasileiro), hacked into the Brazilian president's emails and the emails of two Mexican presidents, monitored German chancellor Angela Merkel's mobile phone, not to speak of those of dozens, possibly hundreds, of other German leaders, and monitored the phone calls of at least thirty-five global leaders (possibly more than a hundred), as well as UN secretary-general Ban Ki-Moon. That's just a partial list of what we've learned so far about the NSA's surveillance programs.

When it comes to the "success" part of the NSA story, you could also play a little numbers game: the NSA has at least thirty-five thousand employees, possibly as many as fifty-five thousand, and an almost $11 billion budget. With up to 70 percent of that budget possibly going to private contractors, we are undoubtedly talking about tens of thousands more "employees" indirectly on the agency's payroll. The Associated Press estimates that there are five hundred thousand employees of private contractors "who have access to the government's most sensitive secrets." In addition to the NSA's mammoth facility in Bluffdale, Utah, since 9/11, according to the *New York Times*, the agency has also built or expanded major data-storage facilities in Georgia, Texas, Colorado, Hawaii, Alaska, and Washington State.

But success, too, can have its downside. There is a small catch when it comes to the NSA's global omniscience. For everything it can, at least theoretically, see, hear, and search, there's one obvious thing the agency's leaders and the rest of the Intelligence Community have proven remarkably un-omniscient about, one thing they clearly have been incapable of taking in—and that's the most essential aspect of the system they are building. Whatever they may have understood about the rest of us, they understood next to nothing about themselves or the real impact of what they were doing, which is why the revelations of Edward Snowden caught them so off guard. Along with the giant Internet corporations, they have been involved in a process aimed at taking away the very notion of a right to privacy in our world. Yet they utterly failed to grasp the basic lesson they have taught the rest of us. If we live in an era of no privacy, there are no exemptions. If, that is, it's an age of no privacy for us, then it's an age of no privacy for them, too.

The word *conspiracy* is an interesting one in this context. It comes from the Latin term *conspirare*, meaning "to breathe the same air." In order to do that, you need to be a small group in a small room. Make yourself the largest surveillance outfit on the planet, hire tens of thousands of private contractors—young computer geeks plunged into a situation that would have boggled the mind of George Orwell—and organize a system of storage and electronic retrieval that puts much at an insider's fingertips, and you've just kissed secrecy good-night and put it to bed for the duration.

There was always going to be an Edward Snowden—or rather Snowdens. And no matter what the NSA and the Obama administration do, no matter what they threaten, no matter how fiercely they attack whistleblowers or who they put away for how long, there will be more. No matter the levels of classification and the desire to throw a penumbra of secrecy over government operations of all sorts, we will eventually know. They have constructed a system potentially riddled with what, in the Cold War days, used to be called "moles." In this case, however, those moles won't be spying for a foreign power but for us. There is no privacy left. That fact of life has been encoded, like so much institutional DNA, in the system they have constructed. They will see us, but in the end, we will see them, too.

Omnipotence?

In light of this, it's worth asking: How's the game of surveillance playing out at the global level? How has success in building such a system translated into policy and power? How useful has it been to have advance information on just what the UN secretary-general will have to say when he visits you at the White House? How helpful is it to store endless tweets, social networking interactions, and phone calls from Egypt when it comes to controlling or influencing actors there, whether the Muslim Brotherhood or the generals? We know that 1,477 "items" from the NSA's PRISM program (which taps into the central servers of nine major US Internet companies) were cited in the president's Daily Briefing in 2012 alone. With all that help, with all that advance notice, with all that insight into the workings of the world from but one of so many NSA programs, just how has Washington been getting along?

All you have to do is look at the world. Long before Snowden walked off with those documents, it was clear things weren't exactly going well. Some breakthroughs in surveillance techniques were, for instance, developed in US war zones in Iraq and Afghanistan, where US intelligence outfits and spies were clearly capable of locating and listening in on insurgent movements in ways never before possible. And yet, we all know what happened in Iraq and is happening in Afghanistan. In both places, omniscience visibly didn't translate into success. When the Arab Spring hit, how prepared was the Obama administration?

In fact, it's reasonable to assume that, while US spymasters and operators were working at the technological frontiers of surveillance and cryptography, their model for success was distinctly antiquated. However unconsciously, they were still living with a World War II–style mindset. Back then, in an all-out military conflict between two sides, listening in on enemy communications had been at least one key to winning the war. Breaking the German Enigma codes meant knowing precisely where the enemy's U-boats were, just as breaking Japan's naval codes ensured victory in the Battle of Midway and elsewhere.

Unfortunately for the NSA and two administrations in Washington, our world isn't so clear-cut. Breaking the codes, whatever codes, isn't going to do the trick. You might be able to pick up every kind of communication in Pakistan or Egypt, but even if you could listen to or read them all (and the NSA doesn't have the linguists or the time to do so), what good would it do you?

Given how Washington has fared since September 12, 2001, the answer would undoubtedly range from not much to none at all—and in the wake of Edward Snowden, it would cross over into the negative. Today, the NSA formula might go something like this: the more communications the agency intercepts, the more it stores, the more it officially knows, the more information it gives those it calls its "external customers" (the White House, the State Department, the CIA, and others), the less omnipotent and more impotent Washington turns out to be.

Once the Edward Snowden revelations began and the vast conspiracy to capture a world of communications was revealed, things only went from bad to worse. Here's just a partial list of some of the casualties from Washington's point of view:

- The first European near-revolt against American power in living memory (former French leader Charles de Gaulle aside), a phenomenon that is still growing across that continent along with an upsurge in distaste for Washington
- A shudder of horror in Brazil and across Latin America, emphasizing a growing distaste for the not-so-good neighbor to the north
- The miraculous transformation of Russia, a country run by a former secret police agent, into a land that provided a haven for an important Western dissident
- A potentially monstrous hit to the Internet giants of Silicon Valley, causing the loss of billions of dollars and possibly their near-monopoly status globally, thanks to the revelation that when you email, tweet, post to Facebook, or do anything else through any of them, you automatically put yourself in the hands of the NSA. Their CEOs are shuddering with worry, as well they should be.

And the list of post-Snowden fallout only seems to be growing.

A First-Place Lineup and a Last-Place Finish

What's perhaps most striking about all this is the inability of the Obama administration and its intelligence bureaucrats to grasp the nature of what's happening to them. For that, they would need to skip those daily briefs from an Intelligence Community that, on the subject, seems clueless, and instead take a clear look at the world.

As a measuring stick for pure tone-deafness in Washington, consider that it took our secretary of state, and so, implicitly, the president, five painful months after Snowden's revelations to finally agree that the NSA had, in certain limited areas, "reached too far." And in response to a global uproar and changing attitudes toward the United States across the planet, their response was laughably modest. According to David Sanger of the *New York Times*, for instance, the administration continued to believe for a remarkably long time that there was "no workable alternative to the bulk collection of huge quantities of 'metadata,' including records of all telephone calls made inside the United States." And despite much dancing around and talk of "reform," in essence they still do.

No one knows what a major state would be like if it radically cut back or even wiped out its intelligence services. No one knows what the planet's sole superpower would be like if it had only one or, for the sake of competition, two major intelligence outfits, rather than seventeen of them, or if those agencies essentially relied on open-source material. In other words, no one knows what the United States would be like if its intelligence agents stopped trying to collect the planet's communications and mainly used their native intelligence to analyze the world. It's hard to imagine, however, that we could be anything but better off.

Amid the news in 2014 about the president's plan to "end" the NSA's gathering of phone metadata (or at least turn it over to the phone companies) and Congress's version of the same—with the devil in the future small print—Paul Waldman made an important point at the *Washington Post*: the larger urge of the national security state to listen in on and gather the communications of everyone everywhere on the planet hasn't changed a bit. Waldman wrote:

> Assuming some version of these proposals passes Congress and gets signed into law, we can be pleased that the bulk collection will be over. But at the risk of becoming a broken record, I have to point out that when it comes to surveillance, phone metadata is nothing compared to what's going to be possible in five or ten or fifteen years as technology advances. And since Obama isn't pulling back because he was forced to by the Supreme Court, which might have set a firm precedent in the process, when the next technological advance comes along that provides some new way to track people that today sounds almost like science fiction, the NSA is going to say, "Ooo, we want that." They may even be working on some new surveillance techniques right now.
>
> What has changed isn't just the different ways the government can watch people, but their ability to watch everyone, then decide later which information is important. Today's news suggests they may be in the process of scaling back one way in which they're doing that right now. But their desire to keep doing it isn't going to go away.

Under the pressure of the ongoing Snowden moment, what they are doing is giving the most modest of ground on one relatively small area of surveillance. And here's my own warning: when a system that hasn't given up reforms itself, watch out! The last time around, in the Watergate era, we ended up with a secret court that decides cases based on only one side of any situation and has created a remarkable body of secret law that could apply to any of us, yet, as citizens of this country, we can know next to nothing about.

Why Washington Has No Learning Curve

In February 2013, the *Washington Post* published a piece by Greg Miller and Karen DeYoung about a reportorial discovery that the *Post*, along with other news outlets including the *New York Times*, had by "an informal arrangement" agreed to suppress (and not even very well) at the request of the Obama administration. More than a year later, and only because the *Times* was breaking the story on the same day (buried in a long investigative piece on drone strikes), the *Post* finally put the news on record. It was half-buried in a piece about a then upcoming confirmation hearing for John O. Brennan, President Obama's nominee to direct the CIA. Until that moment, its editors had done their patriotic duty, urged on by the CIA and the White House, and kept the news from the public. Never mind that the project was so outright loony, given our history, that they should have felt the obligation to publish it instantly with screaming front-page headlines and a lead editorial demanding an explanation.

From another angle, though, you can understand just why the Obama administration and the CIA preferred that the story not come out. Among other things, it had the possibility of making them look like so many horses' asses and, again based on the historical record, it couldn't have been a more dangerous thing to do. It's just the sort of Washington project that brings the word "blowback" instantly and chillingly to mind. It's just the sort of story that should make Americans wonder why we pay billions of dollars to the CIA to think up ideas so tired that you have to wonder what the last two Agency directors, Leon Panetta and David Petraeus, were thinking. (Or if anyone was thinking at all.)

The somewhat less than riveting headline on the *Post* piece was "Brennan Nomination Exposes Criticism on Targeted Killings and Secret Saudi Base." The base story was obviously tacked on at the last second. (There had actually been no "criticism" of that base, since next to nothing was known about it.) It, too, was buried, making its first real appearance only in the tenth paragraph of the piece. According to the *Post*, the CIA received permission from the Saudi government to build one of its growing empire of drone bases in a distant desert region of that kingdom. The purpose was to pursue an already ongoing air war in neighboring Yemen against al-Qaeda on the Arabian Peninsula. The first drone mission from that base seems to have taken off on September 30, 2011, and killed American citizen and al-Qaeda supporter Anwar al-Awlaki. Many more lethal missions have evidently been flown from it since, most or all directed at Yemen in a campaign that notoriously seems to be creating more angry Yemenis and terror recruits than it's killing. So that's the story you waited an extra year to hear from our watchdog press (though for news jockeys, the existence of the base was indeed mentioned in various sly and elliptical ways in the interim by numerous media outlets).

One more bit of information: Brennan, Obama's right-hand counterterrorism guy, who oversaw the president's drone assassination program from an office in the White House basement (you can't take anything away from Washington when it comes to symbolism), was himself a former CIA station chief in Riyadh. The *Post* reported that he worked closely with the Saudis to "gain approval" for the base. So spread the credit around for this one. And note as well that there hasn't been a CIA director with such close ties to a president since William Casey ran the outfit for president Ronald Reagan, and he was the man who got this whole ball of wax rolling by supporting, funding, and arming any Islamic fundamentalist in sight—the more extreme the better—to fight the Soviets in Afghanistan in the 1980s.

Chalmers Johnson used to refer to the CIA as "the president's private army." Now, run by this president's most trusted aide, it once again truly will be so—and air force as well.

To put this secret drone base in a bit of historical context, the Afghan war that Casey funded might be a good place to start. Keep in mind that I'm not talking about the present Afghan war, still ongoing, but our long-forgotten First Afghan War. That was the one where we referred to those Muslim extremists we were arming as "freedom fighters" and President Reagan spoke of them as "the moral equivalent of our Founding Fathers." It was launched to give the Soviets a bloody nose and meant as payback for our bitter defeat in Vietnam less than a decade earlier. And what a bloody nose it would be! Soviet general secretary Mikhail Gorbachev would dub the Soviet disaster there "the bleeding wound," and two years after it ended, the Soviet Union would be gone. I'm talking about the war that, years later, president Jimmy Carter's former national security advisor Zbigniew Brzezinski summed up this way: "What is more important in world history? The Taliban or the collapse of the Soviet empire? Some agitated Muslims or the liberation of Central Europe and the end of the Cold War?"

That's all ancient history and painful to recall now that "agitated Muslims" are a dime a dozen, and we are (as Washington loves to say) in a perpetual global "war" with a "metastasizing" al-Qaeda, an organization that emerged from among our allies in the First Afghan War, as did so many of the extremists now fighting us in Afghanistan.

So how about moving on to a shining moment a decade later: our triumph in the "100-Hour War," in which Washington ignominiously ejected its former ally (and later Adolf Hitler–substitute) Saddam Hussein and his invading Iraqi army from oil-rich Kuwait? Those first hundred hours were, in every sense, a blast. The problems only began to multiply with all the hundred-hour periods that followed for the next decade, what with eternal no-fly zones to patrol and an Iraqi dictator who wouldn't leave the scene.

Maybe, like Washington, we'd do best to skip that episode, too. Let's focus instead on the moment when, in preparation for that war, US troops first landed in Saudi Arabia, that fabulously fundamentalist giant oil reserve; when those hundred hours were over (and Hussein wasn't), they simply moved onto bases and hunkered down for the long haul.

By now, I'm sure some of this is coming back to you: how disturbed, for instance, the rich young Saudi royal and Afghan war veteran Osama bin Laden and al-Qaeda, his young organization, were on seeing those "infidels" based in (or, as they saw it, occupying) the country that held Islam's holiest shrines and pilgrimage sites. I'm sure you can trace al-Qaeda's brief grim history from there: its major operations every couple of years against US targets to back up its demand that those troops depart the kingdom, including the Khobar Towers attack in Saudi Arabia that killed nineteen US airmen in 1996, the destruction of two US embassies in Africa in 1998, and the blowing up of the USS *Cole* in the Yemeni port of Aden in 2000. Finally, of course, there were al-Qaeda's extraordinary attacks of September 11, 2001, which managed—to the reported shock of at least one al-Qaeda figure—to create an apocalyptic-looking landscape of destruction in downtown New York City.

Lusting for revenge, dreaming of a Middle Eastern (or even global) Pax Americana, and eager to loose a military that they believed could eternally dominate any situation, the Bush administration declared a "global war" on terrorism. Only six days after the World Trade Center towers went down, George W. Bush granted the CIA an unprecedented license to wage planet-wide war. By then, it had already presented a plan with a title worthy of a sci-fi film: the "Worldwide Attack Matrix" —with "detailed operations [to come] against terrorists in 80 countries."

This was, of course, a kind of madness. After all, al-Qaeda wasn't a state or even much of an organization; in real terms, it barely existed. So declaring "war" on its scattered minions globally was little short of a bizarre and fantastical act. Yet any other approach to what had happened was promptly laughed out of the American room. And before you could blink, the United States was invading . . . Afghanistan.

After another dazzlingly brief and triumphant campaign, using tiny numbers of American military personnel and CIA operatives (as well as US air power), the first of Washington's you-can't-go-home-again crew marched into downtown Kabul and began hunkering down, building bases, and preparing to stay. One Afghan war, it turned out, hadn't been faintly enough for Washington. And soon, it would be clear that one Iraq war wasn't either. By now, we were in the express lane on the Möbius strip of history.

This should be getting more familiar to you. It might also strike you—though it certainly didn't Washington back in 2002–2003—that there was no reason things should turn out better the second time around. With that new "secret Saudi base" in mind, remember that somewhere in the urge to invade Iraq was the desire to find a place in the heart of the planet's oil lands where the Pentagon would be welcome to create "enduring camps" (please don't call them "permanent bases")—and hang in for enduring decades to come.

So, in early April 2003, invading American troops entered a chaotic Baghdad, a city being looted. ("Stuff happens," commented secretary of defense Donald Rumsfeld infamously in response.) On April 29, Rumsfeld held a news conference with Prince Sultan bin Abdul Aziz, broadcast on Saudi TV, announcing that the United States would pull all its combat troops out of that country. No more garrisons in Saudi Arabia. Ever. US air operations were to move to al-Udeid Air Base in Qatar. As for the rest, there was no need even to mention Iraq. This was two days before President Bush landed a jet, Top Gun–style, on an aircraft carrier off San Diego and—under a White House–produced banner reading "Mission Accomplished"—declared "the end of major combat operations in Iraq." And all's well that ends well, no?

You know the rest, the various predictable disasters that followed (as well as the predictably unpredictable ones). But don't think that, as America's leaders repeat their mistakes endlessly—using varying tactics, ranging from surges to counterinsurgency to special operations raids to drones, all to similar purposes—everything remains the same. Not at all. The repeated invasions, occupations, interventions, drone wars, and the like have played a major role in the unraveling of the Greater Middle East and increasingly of North Africa, as well.

Here is a prediction: keep your eye on the latest drone bases the CIA and the US military are setting up abroad—in Niger, near its border with Mali, for example—and you have a reasonable set of markers for tracing the further destabilization of the planet. Each eerily familiar tactical course change (always treated as a brilliant strategic coup), each application of force, and more things "metastasize."

And so we reach this moment and the news of that two-year-old secret Saudi drone base. You might ask yourself, given the previous history of US bases in that country, why would the CIA or any administration entertain the idea of opening a new US outpost there? Evidently, it's the equivalent of catnip for cats; they just couldn't help themselves.

We don't, of course, know whether they blanked out on recent history or simply dismissed it out of hand, but we do know that once again garrisoning Saudi Arabia seemed too alluring to resist. Without a Saudi base, how could they conveniently strike al-Qaeda wannabes in a neighboring land they were already attacking from the air? And if they weren't to concentrate every last bit of drone power on taking out al-Qaeda types (and civilians) in Yemen, one of the more resource-poor and poverty-stricken places on the planet, why, the next thing you know, al-Qaeda might indeed be ruling a Middle Eastern caliphate. And after that, who knows—the world?

Honestly, could there have been a stupider gamble (again)? This is the sort of thing that helps you understand why conspiracy theories get started—because people in the everyday world just can't accept that, in Washington, dumb and then dumber is the order of the day.

When it comes to that "secret" Saudi base, if truth be told, it does look like a conspiracy—of stupidity. After all, the CIA pushed for and built that base. The White House clearly accepted it as a fine idea. An informal network of key media sources agreed that it really wasn't worth the bother to tell the American people just how stupidly their government was acting. (The managing editor of the *New York Times* explained its suppression by labeling the story nothing more than "a footnote.") And at the public part of the Brennan nomination hearings, none of the members of the Senate Intelligence Committee, which is supposed to provide the CIA and the rest of the US Intelligence Community with what little oversight they get, thought it pertinent to ask a single question about the Saudi base, which was then in the news.

The story was once again buried. Silence reigned. If, in the future, blowback does occur, thanks to the decision to build and use that base, Americans won't make the connection. How could they?

Spies, Traitors, and Defectors in Twenty-First-Century America

Was there anyone growing up like me in the 1950s who didn't know Revolutionary War hero and spy Nathan Hale's last words before the British hanged him: "I only regret that I have but one life to give for my country"? I doubt it. Even today that line, whether historically accurate or not, gives me a chill. Of course, it's harder these days to imagine a use for such a heroically solitary statement—not in an America in which spying and surveillance are boom businesses, and our latest potential Nathan Hales are tens of thousands of corporately hired and trained private intelligence contractors who often don't get closer to the enemy than a computer terminal.

What would Nathan Hale think if you could tell him that the CIA, the preeminent spy agency in the country, has an estimated twenty thousand employees (it won't reveal the exact number, of course)? Or that the National Geospatial-Intelligence Agency, which monitors the nation's spy satellites, has a cast of sixteen thousand housed in a post-9/11, almost $2 billion headquarters in Washington's suburbs? Or that our modern Nathan Hales, multiplying like so many jackrabbits, lack the equivalent of a Britain to spy on?

In the old-fashioned sense, there really is no longer an enemy on the planet. It's true that powers friendly and less friendly still spy on the United States. Remember that ring of suburban-couples-cum-spies the Russians planted here? It was a sophisticated operation that only lacked access to state secrets of any sort and that the FBI rolled up in 2010. But generally speaking, in a single-superpower world, the United States, with no obvious enemy, has been building its own system of global spying and surveillance on a scale never before seen in an effort to keep track of just about everyone on the planet. In other words, Washington is now spy central. It spies not just on potential future enemies but also on its closest allies as if they were enemies. Increasingly, the structure built to do a significant part of that spying is aimed at Americans, too, and on a scale that is no less breathtaking.

Today, for America's spies, Nathan Hale's job comes with health and retirement benefits. Top officials in that world have access to a revolving door into guaranteed lucrative employment at the highest levels of the corporate-surveillance complex—and, of course, for the spy in need of escape, a golden parachute. So when I think about Nathan Hale's famed line, among those hundreds of thousands of American spies and corporate spylings just two Americans come to mind, both charged and one convicted under the Espionage Act, that draconian relic of World War I.

Only one tiny subset of Americans might still be able to cite Hale's words and have them mean anything. Even when Army Private First Class Chelsea (once Bradley) Manning wrote the former hacker who would turn her in, Adrian Lamo, about the possibility that she might find herself in jail for life or be executed, she didn't use those words. But if she had, they would have been appropriate. Former Booz Allen employee Edward Snowden didn't use them in Hong Kong when he discussed the harsh treatment he assumed he would get from his government for revealing the secrets of the NSA, but had he, those words would also have been germane.

The conviction of Manning on six charges under the Espionage Act for releasing secret military and government documents should be a reminder that we are in a rapidly transforming world. It is, however, a world that's increasingly hard to capture accurately because the changes are outpacing the language we have to describe them and so our ability to grasp what is happening. Take the words *spying* and *espionage*. At a national level, you were once a spy who engaged in espionage when, by whatever subterfuge, you gathered the secrets of an enemy, ordinarily an enemy state, for the use of your own country. In recent years, however, those charged under the Espionage Act by the Bush and Obama administrations have not in any traditional sense been spies. None were hired or trained by another power or entity to mine secrets. All had, in fact, been trained either by the US government or an allied corporate entity. All, in their urge to reveal, were whistleblowers who might, in the American past, have been deemed patriots.

None were planning to turn over the information in their possession to an enemy power. Each was trying to make his or her organization, department, or agency conform to proper or better practices or, in the cases of Manning and Snowden, bring to the attention of the American people the missteps and misdeeds of our own government.

To the extent that those whistleblowers were committing acts of espionage, surreptitiously taking secret information from the innards of the national security state for delivery to an "enemy power," that power was "We, the People," the governing power as imagined in the US Constitution. Manning and Snowden each believed that the release of classified documents in his or her possession would empower us, the people, and lead us to question what was being done by the national security state in our name but without our knowledge. In other words, if they were spies, then they were spying on the government for us.

They were, that is, insiders embedded in a vast, increasingly secretive structure that, in the name of protecting us from terrorism, was betraying us in a far deeper way. Both whistleblowers have been termed "traitors" (Manning in military court), while Congressman Peter King called Snowden a "defector," a Cold War term no longer much in use in a one-superpower world. Such words, too, would need new definitions to fit our present reality.

In a sense, Manning and Snowden could be said to have "defected"—from the US secret government to us. However informally or individually, they could nonetheless be imagined as the people's spies. What their cases indicate is that, in this country, the lock-'em-up-and-throw-away-the-key crime of the century is now to spy on the United States for us. That can leave you abused and mistreated in a US military prison, or trapped in Russian exile, or with your career and life in ruins.

In terms of the national security state, spying now has two predominant meanings. It means spying on the world and spying on Americans, both on a massive scale. In the process, that burgeoning structure has become Washington's most precious secret, kept ostensibly from our enemies but actually from us—and even from our elected representatives. The goal of that state, it seems, is to turn the American people into so much absorbable, controllable intelligence data, our identities sliced, diced, and passed around the labyrinthine bureaucracy of the surveillance world, our bytes stored up to be "mined" at their convenience.

Government of the Surveillers, by the Surveillers, for the Surveillers

The truth is that, thanks to our "spies," we know a great deal more about how our American world, our government, actually works, but we still don't know what exactly is being built. Even its creators may be at sea when it comes to what exactly they are in the process of constructing. They want us to trust them, but we the people shouldn't put our trust in the generals, high-level bureaucrats, and spooks who don't even blink when they lie to our representatives, pay no price for doing so, and are continuing to create a world that is, and is meant to be, beyond our control.

We lack words for what is happening to us. We still have to name it. But it is at least clearer that our world, our society, is becoming ever more imperial in nature, reflecting in part the way our post-9/11 wars have come home. With its widening economic inequalities, the United States is increasingly a society of the rulers and the ruled, the surveillers and the surveilled. Those surveillers have hundreds of thousands of spies to keep track of us and others on this planet, and no matter what they do, no matter what lines they cross, no matter how egregious their acts may be, they are never punished for them, not even losing their jobs. We, on the other hand, have a tiny number of volunteer surveillers on our side. The minute they make themselves known or are tracked down by the national security state, they automatically lose their jobs—and that's only the beginning of the punishments levied against them.

Those who run our new surveillance state have not the slightest hesitation about sacrificing us on the altar of their plans—all for the greater good, as they define it.

This, of course, has nothing whatsoever to do with any imaginable definition of democracy or the long-gone republic. This is part of the new way of life of imperial America in which a government of the surveillers, by the surveillers, for the surveillers shall not perish from the earth.

Those who watch us—they would undoubtedly say "watch over," as in protect—are no Nathan Hales. Their version of his line might be: *I only regret that I have but one life to give for my country—yours.*

FIVE

Definitions for a New Age

In the months after September 11, 2001, it was regularly said that "every-thing" had changed. It's a claim long forgotten, buried in everyday American life. Still, if you think about it, in the decade-plus that followed—the years of the PATRIOT Act, "enhanced interrogation techniques," "black sites," robot assassination campaigns, extraordinary renditions, the Abu Ghraib photos, the Global War on Terror, and the first cyberwar in history—much did change in ways that should still stun us.

Unfortunately, the language we use to describe the world of the national security state is still largely stuck in the pre-9/11 era. No wonder, for example, it's hard to begin to grasp the staggering size and shape-shifting nature of the world of secret surveillance that Edward Snowden's revelations have uncovered. If there are no words available to capture the world that is watching us, all of us, we've got a problem.

In ancient China, when a new dynasty came to power, it would per-form a ceremony called "the rectification of names." The idea was that the previous dynasty had, in part, fallen because a gap, a chasm had opened between reality and the names available to describe it. Consider this chapter, then, a first attempt to "rectify" American names in the era of the ascendant global security state.

Creating a new dictionary of terms is, of course, an awesome undertaking. From the moment work on it began, the full ten-volume *Oxford English Dictionary* famously took seventy-one years to first appear. Here, however, is an initial glimpse at a modest selection of newly rectified definitions.

Secret: Anything of yours the government takes possession of and classifies.

Classification: The process of declaring just about any document produced by any branch of the US government—more than 92 million of them in 2011—unfit for unclassified eyes. (This term may, in the near future, be retired once no documents produced within, or captured by, the government and its intelligence agencies can be seen or read by anyone not given special clearance.)

Surveillance: Here's looking at you, kid.

Whistleblower: A homegrown terrorist.

Leak: Information homegrown terrorists slip to journalists to undermine the American way of life and aid and abet the enemy. A recent example would be the documents Edward Snowden leaked to the media. According to two unnamed US intelligence officials speaking to the Associated Press, "[M]embers of virtually every terrorist group, including core al-Qaida, are attempting to change how they communicate, based on what they are reading in the media [of Snowden's revelations], to hide from U.S. surveillance." A clarification: two anonymous intelligence officials communicating obviously secret material to AP reporter Kimberly Dozier does not qualify as a "leak," but as necessary information for Americans to absorb. In addition, those officials undoubtedly had further secret intelligence indicating that their information, unlike Snowden's, would be read only by Americans and ignored by al-Qaeda-style terrorists who will not change their actions based on it. As a result, this cannot qualify as aiding or abetting the enemy.

Journalist: Someone who aids and abets terrorists, traitors, defectors, and betrayers hidden within our government as they work to accomplish their grand plan to undermine the security of the country.

Source: Someone who tells a journalist what no one, other than the NSA, the CIA, the DIA, the FBI, the DHS, and similar outfits should know (see "secret"). Such a source will be hunted down and prosecuted to the full extent of the law—or beyond (see "Espionage Act"). Fortunately, as Associated Press president Gary Pruitt pointed out, thanks to diligent government action, sources are ever harder to come by. "Some of our longtime trusted sources have become nervous and anxious about talking to us, even on stories that aren't about national security," he noted. "And in some cases, government employees that we once checked in with regularly will no longer speak to us by phone, and some are reluctant to meet in person." Someday, sources may no longer exist. When an unnamed administration official offers information privately to a journalist, however, he or she is not a source—just too humble to take credit for feeding us crucial information needed to understand the complex world we live in.

Blood: This is what leakers have on their hands. A leak, embarrassing the national security state, endangers careers (bloody enough) and, by definition, US lives. Thus Chelsea Manning, in releasing classified State Department and US military documents to WikiLeaks, and Edward Snowden, in releasing NSA secrets to the *Guardian*, the *Washington Post*, the *South China Morning Post*, and *Der Spiegel*, have blood on their hands. We know this because top US officials have told us so. Note that it does not matter if no deaths or physical injuries can directly be traced to or attributed to their actions. This is, however, a phrase with very specific and limited application. American political and military officials who launch aggressive wars, allow torture, kidnapping, and abuse, run drone assassination programs, and the like do not have blood on their hands. It is well known that they are bloodless.

Insider Threat Program: The name of an Obama administration initiative to promote patriotism inside the government. Its goal is to encourage federal employees to become more patriotic by picking up on clues that potentially traitorous coworkers might consider leaking classified information to the enemy (see "journalist"). Government managers, again to promote love of country, are encouraged to crack down on any employees who are found not to have been patriotic enough to report their suspicions about said coworkers. (Words never to be associated with this program: *informer, rat,* or *fink.*)

Patriot: Americans are by nature "patriots." If they love their country too well like (to take but one example) former vice president Dick Cheney, they are "super-patriots." Both of these are good things. Foreigners cannot be patriots. If they exhibit an unseemly love of country, they are "nationalists." If that love goes beyond all bounds, they are "ultranationalists." These are both bad things.

Espionage Act: A World War I law focused on aiding and abetting the enemy in wartime that has been used more than twice as often by the Obama administration as by all previous administrations combined. Since 9/11, the United States has, of course, been continuously "at war," which makes the act handy indeed. Whistleblowers automatically violate the act when they bring to public attention information Americans really shouldn't bother their pretty little heads about. It may be what an investigative reporter (call him "Glenn Greenwald") violates when he writes stories based on classified information from the national security state not leaked by the White House.

Trust: What you should have in the national security state and the president to do the right thing, no matter how much power they accrue, how many secrets of yours or anybody else's they gather, or what other temptations might exist. Americans can make mistakes, but by their nature (see "patriots"), with the exception of whistleblowers, they can never mean to do wrong (unlike the Chinese or the Russians). As the president has pointed out, "Every member of Congress has been briefed on [the NSA's] telephone program and the intelligence committees have been briefed on the Internet program, with both approved and reauthorized by bipartisan committees since 2006. . . . If people don't trust Congress and the judiciary then I think we are going to have some problems here."

Truth: The most important thing on earth, hence generally classified. It is something that cannot be spoken by national security officials in open session before Congress without putting the American people in danger. As director of national intelligence James Clapper has made clear, however, any official offering such public testimony can at least endeavor to speak in "the least untruthful manner" possible; that is, in the nearest approximation of truth that remains unclassified in the post-9/11 era.

US Constitution: A revered piece of paper that no one pays much actual attention to any more, especially if it interferes with powers the government claims it must exercise in order to protect the "homeland" from terrorism.

Amendments: Retrospectively unnecessary additions to the US Constitution guaranteeing a series of things, some of which may now put us in peril (examples: the First Amendment, the Fourth Amendment, the Fifth Amendment's "due process" clause). Fortunately, amendments turn out to be easy enough to effectively amend within the national security state itself.

Checks and balances: No longer applicable, except to your bank statement.

The fourth branch of government: Classically, the United States had three branches of government (the executive, legislative, and judicial), which were to check and balance one another so that power would never become centralized and unopposed in a single branch. The founding fathers, however, were less farsighted than many give them credit for. They hadn't a clue that a fourth branch of government, the national security state, would arise, dedicated to the centralization of power in an atmosphere of total secrecy. In the post-9/11 years, it has significantly absorbed the other three branches.

Congressional oversight: When a congressional representative forgets to do something. (Historical note: this phrase once had another meaning, but since 9/11, years in which Congress never heard a wish of the national security state that it didn't grant, no one can quite remember what it was.)

National Security Agency (NSA): A top-secret spy outfit once nicknamed "No Such Agency" because its very existence was not acknowledged by the US government. It is now known as "No Such Agency" because its work has been outsourced to high-priced high-school dropouts or "No Snowden Anywhere" because it couldn't locate the world's most famous leaker.

American security (or safety): The national security state works hard to offer its citizens a guarantee of safety from the nightmare of terror attacks, which since 9/11 have killed more Americans than shark attacks but not much else. For this guarantee, there is, of course, a necessary price to be paid. You, the citizen and taxpayer, must fund your own safety from terrorism (to the tune of trillions of dollars heading into the national security budget) and cede rights that were previously yours. You must, for instance, allow yourself to be "seen" in myriad ways by the national security state, must allow for the possibility that you could be assassinated without "due process" to keep this country safe, and so on. This is called "striking a balance" between American liberty and security. Or as the president put it, "You can't have 100 percent security and also then have 100 percent privacy and zero inconvenience. . . . We're going to have to make some choices as a society. . . . There are trade-offs involved." By the way, in return for your pliancy, this guarantee does not extend to keeping you safe from cars, guns, cigarettes, food-borne diseases, natural disasters of any sort, and so on.

The Global War on You (GWOY): This term, not yet in the language, is designed to replace a post-9/11 Bush administration name, the Global War on Terror (GWOT), sometimes also called World War IV by neocons. GWOT was famously retired by President Obama and his top officials, turning the ongoing global war being fought on distant battlefields and in the shadows into a nameless one. That may, however, change. You are, after all, being called to the colors in a war on . . . you. You, after all, are the central figure in and the key to GWOY and the basis upon which the new global security state will continue to be built.

The American Exceptionalism Sweepstakes

"But when, with modest effort and risk, we can stop children from being gassed to death, and thereby make our own children safer over the long run, I believe we should act. That's what makes America different. That's what makes us exceptional. With humility, but with resolve, let us never lose sight of that essential truth."
—Barack Obama, address to the nation on Syria,
September 10, 2013

Let's be Americans, which means being exceptional, which also means being honest in ways inconceivable to the rest of humanity. So here's the truth of it: the American exceptionalism sweepstakes really do matter. A lot.

Barack Obama is only the latest in a jostling crowd—of presidential candidates, presidential wannabes, major politicians, and minor figures of every sort, not to speak of a raging horde of neocons and pundits galore—who have felt compelled in recent years to tell us and the world just how exceptional the last superpower really is. They tend to emphasize our ability to use this country's overwhelming power, especially of the military variety, for the global good—to save children and other deserving innocents. This particularly American aptitude for doing good forcibly, by killing others, is considered an incontestable fact of earthly life needing no proof. It is well known, especially among our leading politicians, that Washington has the ability to wield its military strength in ways that are unimaginably superior to any other power on the planet.

The bragging rights to American exceptionalism are no small matter. It should hardly be surprising, then, how visceral is the response when any foreigner—say, Russian president Vladimir Putin—decides to appropriate the term and uses it to criticize us. How visceral? Well, the sort of visceral that, as Democratic senator Bob Menendez put it, leaves us barely repressing the urge to "vomit."

Now, it's not that we can't take a little self-criticism. If you imagine an over-muscled, over-armed guy walking into a room and promptly telling you and anyone else in earshot how exceptionally good he is when it comes to targeting his weapons, and you notice a certain threatening quality about him, and maybe a hectoring, lecturing tone in his voice, it's possible that you might be intimidated by or irritated with him. You might think: narcissist, braggart, or blowhard. If you were the president of Russia, you might say, "It is extremely dangerous to encourage people to see themselves as exceptional, whatever the motivation."

Yes, if you're a foreigner, this country is easy enough to misunderstand, make fun of, or belittle. Still, that didn't stop the president from proudly bringing up our exceptionalism in his address on the need for a US military response to the use of chemical weapons by the Syrian military. He recommended launching a "limited strike," assumedly Tomahawk missiles heading Damascus-ward, to save Syria's children, and he made sure the world knew that such an attack would be no passing thing. ("Let me make something clear: the United States military doesn't do pinpricks.")

Then, in mid-speech, in a fashion that was nothing short of exceptional (if you were considering the internal logic of the address), he suddenly took another approach entirely. But don't let foreign criticism blind you to the power of the president's imagery. In this century, as he suggested then and in an address to the United Nations two weeks later, American exceptionalism has always had to do with Washington's ability to use its power for the greater planetary good. Since, in the last decade-plus, power and military power have become essentially synonymous in Washington, the pure goodness of firing missiles or dropping bombs has been sanctified.

On that basis, it's indisputable that the bragging rights to exceptionalism are Washington's. For those who need proof, what follows are just eight ways (among so many more) that you can proudly make the case for our exceptional status, should you happen to stumble across, say, President Putin, still blathering on, post–Crimean annexation, about how unexceptional we are.

1. What other country could have invaded Iraq, hardly knowing the difference between a Sunni and a Shiite, and managed to successfully set off a brutal sectarian civil war and ethnic cleansing campaign between the two sects that would subsequently go regional, whose casualty counts have tipped into the hundreds of thousands, and which is now bouncing back on Iraq? What other great power would have launched its invasion with plans to garrison that country for decades

and with the larger goal of subduing neighboring Iran, only to slink away eight years later, leaving behind a Shiite government in Baghdad that was a firm ally of Iran? And in what other country could leaders, viewing these consequences and knowing our part in them, contemplate sending in the missiles and bombers again, this time perhaps into Syria or Iran? Who in the world would dare claim that this isn't an unmatchable record?

2. What other country could magnanimously spend $4 to $6 trillion on two "good wars" in Afghanistan and Iraq against lightly armed minority insurgencies without winning or accomplishing a thing? And that's not even counting the funds sunk into the Global War on Terror and sideshows in places like Pakistan, Somalia, and Yemen, or the staggering sums that, since 9/11, have been poured directly into the national security state. How many countries, possessing "the finest fighting force in the history of the world," could have engaged in endless armed conflicts and interventions from the 1960s on and, except in unresisting Panama and tiny Grenada, never managed to definitively win anything?

3. And talking about exceptional records, what other military could have brought an estimated 3.1 million pieces of equipment—ranging from tanks and Humvees to port-a-potties, coffee makers, and computers— into Iraq and then transported most of them out again (while destroying the rest or turning them over to the Iraqis)? Similarly, in an Afghanistan where the US military is now drawing down its forces and has already destroyed "more than 170 million pounds worth of vehicles and other military equipment," what other force would have decided ahead of time to shred, dismantle, or simply discard $7 billion worth of equipment (about 20 percent of what it had brought into the country)? Even the general in charge calls this "the largest retrograde mission in history." To put that in context: What other military would be capable of carrying a total consumer society right down to PXs, massage parlors, boardwalks, Internet cafes, and food courts to war? Let's give credit where it's due: we're not just talking retrograde here, we're talking exceptionally retrograde!

4. What other military could, in a mere few years in Iraq, have built a staggering 505 bases, ranging from combat outposts to ones the size of small American towns with their own electricity generators, water purifiers, fire departments, fast food restaurants, and even miniature golf courses, at a cost of unknown billions of dollars and then, only a few years later, have abandoned all of them, dismantling some, turning others over to the Iraqi military or into ghost towns, and leaving yet others to be looted and stripped? And what other military, in the same time period thousands of miles away in Afghanistan, could have built more than 450 bases, sometimes even hauling in the building materials, only now to be dismantling them in the same fashion? If those aren't exceptional feats, what are?

5. In a world where it's hard to get anyone to agree on anything, the covert campaign of drone strikes that George W. Bush launched and Barack Obama escalated in Pakistan's tribal areas stands out. Those hundreds of strikes not only caused significant numbers of civilian casualties including children, while helping to destabilize a sometime ally, but also created the basis for opinion polls in which a Ripley's-Believe-It-or-Not!-style 97 percent of Pakistanis offered them an emphatic thumbs-down. Is there another country on the planet capable of mobilizing such loathing? Stand proud, America!

6. And what other power could have secretly and illegally kidnapped at least 136 suspected terrorists—some, in fact, innocent of any such acts or associations—off the streets of global cities, as well as from the backlands of the planet? What other nation could have mustered a "coalition of the willing" of fifty-four countries to lend a hand in its "rendition" operations? We're talking about more than a quarter of the nations on Earth! And that isn't all. Oh, no. Can you imagine another country capable of setting up a genuinely global network of "black sites" and borrowed prisons (with local torturers on hand), places to stash and abuse those kidnappees (and other prisoners) in locations ranging from Poland to Thailand, Romania to Afghanistan, Egypt and Uzbekistan to US Navy ships on the high seas, not to speak of that jewel in the crown of offshore prisons, Guantánamo? Such illegality on such a global scale simply can't be matched. And

don't even get me started on torture. (It's fine for us to take pride in our exceptionalist tradition, but you don't want to pile on.)

7. Or how about the way the State Department, to the tune of $750 million, constructed in Baghdad the largest, most expensive embassy compound on the planet—a 104-acre, Vatican-sized citadel with twenty-seven blast-resistant buildings, an indoor pool, basketball courts, and a fire station, which was to operate as a command-and-control center for our ongoing garrisoning of Iraq and the region? Now the garrisons are gone, and the embassy, its staff cut, is a global white elephant. But what an exceptional elephant. Think of it as a modern American pyramid, a tomb in which lie buried the dreams of establishing a Pax Americana in the Greater Middle East. Honestly, what other country could hope to match that sort of memorial thousands of miles from home?

8. Or what about this? Between 2002 and 2011, the US government poured at least $51 billion into building up a vast Afghan military. Another $11 billion was dedicated to the task in 2012, with almost $6 billion more for 2013. Washington has also sent in a legion of trainers tasked with turning that force into an American-style fighting outfit. At the time Washington began building it up, the Afghan army was reportedly a heavily illiterate, drug-taking, corrupt, and ineffective force that lost one-third to one-half of its personnel to casualties, non-reenlistment, and desertion in any year. In 2012, the latest date for which we have figures, the Afghan security forces were still a heavily illiterate, drug-taking, corrupt, and inefficient outfit that was losing about one-third of its personnel annually (a figure that may even be on the rise). The United States and its NATO allies are committed to spending $4.1 billion annually on the same project after the withdrawal of their combat forces in 2014. Tell me that isn't exceptional.

No one, of course, loves a braggart. So, easy as it might be to supplement these eight examples with others, the winner of the exceptionalism sweepstakes is already obvious. In other words, this is a moment for exceptional modesty, which means that only one caveat needs to be added to the above record.

I'm talking about actual property rights to "American exceptionalism." It's a phrase often credited to a nineteenth-century foreigner, the French traveler Alexis de Tocqueville. As it happens, however, the man who seems to have first used the full phrase was Russian dictator Joseph Stalin. In 1929, when the United States was showing few signs either of a proletarian uprising or of fulfilling Karl Marx's predictions, and American Communists were claiming that the country had unique characteristics that left it unready for revolution, Stalin began denouncing "the heresy of American exceptionalism." Outside the US Communist Party, the phrase only gained popular traction here in the Reagan years. Now, it has become as American as barbeque potato chips. If, for instance, as has been claimed, the phrase had never before been used in a presidential debate, the candidates couldn't stop spouting it in 2012.

Still, history does give Vladimir Putin a claim to the use of the phrase, however stomach-turning that may be for various members of Congress. But maybe, in its own way, its origins only attest to . . . well, American exceptionalism. Somehow, through pureness of motive and the shining radiance of the way we exercise power, Washington's politicians have taken words wielded negatively by one of the great monsters of history and made them the signature phrase of American greatness. How exceptional!

We're Number One . . .
in Obliterating Wedding Parties

The headline—"Bride and Boom!"—was spectacular, if you think killing people in distant lands is a blast and a half. Of course, you have to imagine that smirk line in giant black letters with a monstrous exclamation point covering most of the bottom third of the front page of the Rupert Murdoch–owned *New York Post*. The reference was to a caravan of vehicles on its way to or from a wedding in Yemen that was eviscerated, evidently by one of those "surgical" US drone strikes of which Washington is so proud. As a report from the scene put it, "Scorched vehicles and body parts were left scattered on the road."

It goes without saying that such a headline could only be applied to dangerous foreigners—"terror" or "al-Qaeda suspects"—in distant lands whose deaths carry a certain quotient of weirdness and even amusement with them. Try to imagine the equivalent for the Newtown massacre the day after Adam Lanza walked into Sandy Hook Elementary School and began killing children and teachers. Since even the *New York Post* wouldn't do such a thing, let's posit that the *Yemen Post* did, that playing off the phrase "head of the class," its headline was: "Dead of the Class!" (with that same giant exclamation point). It would be sacrilege. The media would descend. The tastelessness of Arabs would be denounced all the way up to the White House. You'd hear about the callousness of foreigners for days.

And were a wedding party to be obliterated on a highway anywhere in the United States on the way to, say, a rehearsal dinner, whatever the cause, it would be a 24/7 tragedy. Our lives would be filled with news of it. Count on that.

But a bunch of Arabs in a country few in the United States had ever heard of before we started sending in the drones? No such luck. So, if you're a Murdoch tabloid, it's open season, no consequences guaranteed. As it happens, "Bride and Boom!" isn't even an original. It turns out to be a stock *Post* headline. Google it and you'll find that, since 9/11, the paper had used it at least twice before, and never for the good guys: once in 2005, for "the first bomb-making husband and wife," two Palestinian newlyweds arrested by the Israelis, and once in 2007, for a story about a "bride," decked out in a "princess-style wedding gown," with her "groom." Their car was stopped at a checkpoint in Iraq by our Iraqis, and both of them turned out to be male "terrorists" in a "nutty nuptial party." Ba-boom!

As it happened, the article by Andy Soltis accompanying the *Post* headline began quite inaccurately. "A U.S. drone strike targeting al-Qaeda militants in Yemen," went the first line, "took out an unlikely target on Thursday—a wedding party heading to the festivities."

Soltis can, however, be forgiven his ignorance. In this country, no one bothers to count up wedding parties wiped out by US airpower. If they did, Soltis would have known that the accurate line, given the history of US war-making since December 2001, when the first party of Afghan wedding revelers was wiped out (only two women survived), would have been: "A US drone . . . took out a likely target."

After all, by my count, this is at least the eighth wedding party reportedly massacred totally or in part since the Afghan war began and it extends the extermination of wedding celebrants from the air to a third country—six destroyed in Afghanistan, one in Iraq, and now the first in Yemen. And in all those years, reporters covering these "incidents" never seem to notice that similar events had occurred previously. Sometimes whole wedding parties were slaughtered, sometimes just the bride or groom's parties were hit. Estimated total dead from the eight incidents: almost three hundred Afghans, Iraqis, and Yemenis. And keep in mind that, in these years, weddings haven't been the only rites hit. US airpower has struck gatherings ranging from funerals to a baby-naming ceremony.

The only thing that made the Yemeni incident unique was the drone. The previous strikes were reportedly by piloted aircraft.

Non-tabloid papers were far more polite in their headlines and accounts, though they did reflect utter confusion about what had happened in a distant part of distant Yemen. The wedding caravan of vehicles was going to a wedding—or coming back. Fifteen were definitively dead. Or eleven. Or thirteen. Or fourteen. Or seventeen. The attacking plane had aimed for al-Qaeda targets and hit the wedding party "by mistake." Or al-Qaeda "suspects" had been among the wedding party, though all reports agreed that innocent wedding-goers died. Accounts of what happened from Yemeni officials differed, even as that country's parliamentarians demanded an end to the US drone campaign in their country. The Obama administration refused to comment. It was generally reported that this strike, like others before it, had—strangely enough—upset Yemenis and made them more amenable to the propaganda of al-Qaeda on the Arabian Peninsula.

In the end, reports on a wedding slaughter in a distant land are generally relegated to the inside pages of the paper and passing notice on the TV news, an event instantly trumped by almost anything whatsoever—a school shooting anywhere in the United States, snowstorms across the Northeast, you name it—and promptly buried and forgotten.

And yet, in a country that tends to value records, this represents record-making material. After all, what are the odds of knocking off all or parts of eight wedding parties in the space of a little more than a decade (assuming, of course, that the destruction of other wedding parties or the killing of other wedding-goers in America's distant war zones hasn't gone unreported). If the Taliban or the Iranians or the North Koreans had piled up such figures—and indeed the Taliban has done wedding damage via roadside bombs and suicide bombers—we would know just what to think of them. We would classify them as barbarians, savages, evildoers.

You might imagine that such a traffic jam of death and destruction would at least merit some longer-term attention, thought, analysis, and discussion here. But with the rarest of exceptions, it's nowhere to be found, right, left, or center, in Washington or Topeka, in everyday conversation or think-tank speak. And keep in mind that we're talking about a country where the slaughter of innocents—in elementary schools, high schools, colleges and universities, workplaces and movie theaters, parking lots and naval shipyards—is given endless attention, carefully totaled up, discussed, and debated until "closure" is reached (or the next domestic bit of carnage comes along).

And yet no one here even thinks to ask how this many wedding parties in foreign lands could be so repeatedly taken out. Is the United States simply targeting weddings purposely? Not likely. Could it reflect the fact that, despite all the discussion of the "surgical precision" of American airpower, pilots have remarkably little idea what's really going on below them or who exactly, in lands where American intelligence must be half-blind, they're aiming at? That, at least, seems likely.

Or if "they" gather in certain regions, does American intelligence just assume that the crowd must be "enemy" in nature? (As an American general said about a wedding party attacked in Western Iraq, "How many people go to the middle of the desert . . . to hold a wedding 80 miles from the nearest civilization?") Or is it possible that, in our global war zones, a hint that enemy "suspects" might be among a party of celebrants means that the party itself is fair game, that it's open season no matter who might be in the crowd?

In this same spirit, the US drone campaigns are said to launch what in drone-speak are called "signature strikes"—that is, strikes not against identified individuals, but against "a pre-identified 'signature' of behavior that the U.S. links to militant activity." In other words, the United States launches drone strikes against groups or individuals whose behavior simply fits a "suspect" category: young men of military age carrying weapons, for instance (in areas where carrying a weapon may be the norm no matter who you are). In a more general sense, however, the obliterated wedding party may be the true signature strike of the post-9/11 era of American war-making, the strike that should, but never will, remind Americans that the war on terror was and remains, for others in distant lands, a war *of* terror, a fearsome creation to which we are conveniently blind.

Consider it a record. For the period since September 11, 2001, we're number one—in obliterating wedding parties. In those years, whether we care to know it or not, "till death do us part" has gained a far grimmer meaning.

Remotely Piloted War

In the American mind, if Apple made weapons, they would undoubtedly be drones, those remotely piloted planes getting such great press here. They have generally been greeted as if they were the sleekest of new iPhones, armed with missiles.

When the first American drone assassins burst onto the global stage early in the last decade, they caught most of us by surprise, especially because they seemed to come from some wild sci-fi novel. Ever since, they've been touted in the media as the shiniest presents under the American Christmas tree of war, the perfect weapons to solve our problems when it comes to evildoers lurking in the global badlands.

And can you blame Americans for their love affair with the drone? Who wouldn't be wowed by the most technologically advanced, futuristic, no-pain-all-gain weapon around?

But something far less exotic is really at work here. What does a drone do? Like a modern car factory, it replaces a pilot, a skilled job that takes significant training, with robotics and an outsourced, degraded version of the same job. In this case, the "offshore" location that job headed for wasn't China or Mexico but a military base in the United States, where a guy with a joystick, trained in a hurry and sitting at a computer monitor, is "piloting" that plane. And given our experience with the hemorrhaging of good jobs in the United States, who will be surprised to discover that, by 2011, the US Air Force was already training more drone "pilots" than actual fighter and bomber pilots combined?

That's one way drones are something other than the futuristic sci-fi wonders we imagine them to be. But there's another way that they have been heading for the American "homeland" for four decades, and it has next to nothing to do with technology, advanced or otherwise.

In a sense, drone war might be thought of as the most natural form of war for the all-volunteer military. To understand why that's so, we need to head back to a crucial decision implemented just as the Vietnam War was ending.

It's true that, in the wake of grinding wars that have also been debacles, the US military is in ratty shape. Its equipment needs refurbishing and its troops are worn down. The stress of endlessly repeated tours of duty in war zones, brain injuries and other wounds caused by the roadside bombs that have often replaced a visible enemy on the "battlefield," suicide rates that can't be staunched, rising sexual violence within the military, increasing crime rates around military bases, and all the other strains and pains of unending war have taken their toll.

Still, ours remains an intact, unrebellious, professional military. If you really want to see a force on its last legs, you need to go back to the Vietnam era. In 1971, in *Armed Forces Journal*, Colonel Robert D. Heinl, Jr., author of a history of the Marine Corps, wrote of "widespread conditions among American forces in Vietnam that have only been exceeded in this century by the French Army's Nivelle mutinies of 1917 and the collapse of the Tsarist armies [of Russia] in 1916 and 1917." The US military in Vietnam and at bases in the United States and around world was essentially at the edge of rebellion. Disaffection with an increasingly unpopular war on the Asian mainland, rejected by ever more Americans and emphatically protested at home, had infected the military, which was, after all, made up significantly of draftees.

Desertion rates were rising, as was drug use. In the field, "search and evade" (a mocking, descriptively accurate replacement for "search and destroy") operations were becoming commonplace. "Fraggings"—attacks on unpopular officers—had doubled. ("Word of the deaths of officers will bring cheers at troop movies or in bivouacs of certain units.") And according to Colonel Heinl, there were then as many as 144 antiwar "underground newspapers" published by or aimed at soldiers. At the moment he was writing, in fact, the antiwar movement in the United States was being spearheaded by a rising tide of disaffected Vietnam veterans speaking out against their war and the way they had fought it.

In this fashion, an American citizens' army, a draft military, had reached its limits and was voting with its feet against an imperial war. This was democracy in action transferred to the battlefield and the military base. And it was deeply disturbing to the US high command, which had, by then, lost faith in the future possibilities of a draft army. In fact, faced with ever more ill-disciplined troops, the military's top commanders had clearly concluded: never again.

So on the very day the Paris Peace Accords were signed in January 1973, officially signaling the end of US involvement in Vietnam (though not quite its actual end), president Richard Nixon also signed a decree ending the draft. It was an admission of the obvious: war, American-style, as it had been practiced since World War II, had lost its hold on young minds.

There was no question that US military and civilian leaders intended, at that moment, to sever war and war-making from an aroused citizenry. In that sense, they glimpsed something of the future they meant to shape, but even they couldn't have guessed just where American war would be heading. Army chief of staff General Creighton Abrams, for instance, actually thought he was curbing the future rashness of civilian leaders by—as Andrew Bacevich explained in his book *The New American Militarism*—"making the active army operationally dependent on the reserves." In this way, no future president could commit the country to a significant war "without first taking the politically sensitive and economically costly step of calling up America's 'weekend warriors.'"

Abrams was wrong, of course, though he ensured that, decades hence, the reserves, too, would suffer the pain of disastrous wars once again fought on the Eurasian mainland. Still, whatever the generals and the civilian leaders didn't know about the effects of their acts then, the founding of the All-Volunteer Force (AVF) may have been the single most important decision made by Washington in the post-Vietnam era of the foreshortened American Century.

Today, few enough even remember that moment in 1973 and far fewer have considered its import. Yet, historically speaking, that severing of war from the populace might be said to have ended an almost two-century-old democratic experiment in fusing the mobilized citizen and the mobilized state in wartime. It had begun with the *levée en masse* during the French Revolution, which sent roused citizens to the front to save the republic and spread their democratic fervor abroad. Behind them stood a mobilized population ready to sacrifice anything for the republic (and all too soon, of course, for the empire). It turned out, however, that the drafted citizen had his limits and so, almost two hundred years later, another aroused citizenry and its soldiers, home front and war front, were to be pacified by being put out to pasture, while the empire's wars were to be left to the professionals. An era was ending, even if no one noticed. (As a result, if you're in the mood to indulge in irony, citizens' war would be left to the guerrillas of the world, which in our era has largely meant to fundamentalist religious sects.) Just calling in the professionals and ushering out the amateurs wasn't enough, though, to make the decision truly momentous. Another choice had to be married to it. The debacle that was Vietnam—or what, as the 1970s progressed, began to be called "the Vietnam Syndrome" (as if the American people had been struck by some crippling psychic disease)—could have sent Washington, and so the nation, off on another course entirely.

The United States could have retreated, however partially, from the world to lick its wounds. Instead, the country's global stance as the "leader of the free world" and its role as self-appointed global policeman were never questioned. Nor was the global military-basing policy that underlay it. In the midst of the Cold War, from Indonesia to Latin America, Japan to the Middle East, no diminution of US imperial dreams was ever seriously considered.

The decision not to downsize the US global military presence after Vietnam fused with the decision to create a military that would free Washington from worrying about what the troops might think. Soon enough, as Bacevich wrote, the new AVF would be made up of "highly trained, handsomely paid professionals who (assuming that the generals concur with the wishes of the political leadership) [would] go anywhere without question to do the bidding of the commander-in-chief." It would, in fact, open the way for a new kind of militarism at home and abroad.

The Arrival of the Warrior Corporation

In the wake of Vietnam, the wars ceased and, for a few years, war imagery was swept out of American popular culture. When it returned, the dog-fights would be in outer space. (Think *Star Wars*.) In the meantime, a kind of stunned silence, a feeling of defeat, descended on the American polity—but not for long. In the 1980s, the years of Ronald Reagan's presidency, American-style war was carefully rebuilt, this time to new specifications. Reagan declared Vietnam "a noble cause," and a newly professionalized military, purged of malcontents and rebels, once again began invading small countries (Grenada, Panama). At the same time, the Pentagon was investing thought and planning into how to put the media (blamed for defeat in Vietnam) in its rightful place and so give the public the war news it deserved. In the process, reporters were first restrained from, then "pooled" in, and finally "embedded" in the war effort, while retired generals were sent into TV newsrooms like so many play-by-play analysts on *Monday Night Football* to narrate our wars as they were happening. Meanwhile, the public was simply sidelined.

Year by year, war became an ever more American activity and yet grew ever more remote from most Americans. The democratic citizen with a free mind and the ability to rebel had been sent home and was then demobilized on that home front as well. As a result, despite the endless post-9/11 gab about honoring and supporting the troops, a mobilized "home front" sacrificing for those fighting in their name became a relic of history in a country whose leaders had begun boasting of having "the greatest military the world has ever seen."

It wasn't, however, that no one was mobilizing. In the space vacated by the citizen, mobilization continued, just in a different fashion. Ever more mobilized, for instance, would be the powers of Big Science and the academy in the service of the Pentagon, the weapons makers, and the corporation. Over the years, the "professional" army, that "all volunteer" force, began to change as well. From the 1990s on, in a way that would have been inconceivable for a draft army, it began to be privatized—fused, that is, into the corporate way of war and profit. War would now be fought not for or by the citizen, but quite literally for and by Lockheed Martin, Halliburton, KBR, DynCorp, Triple Canopy, and Blackwater (later Xe, even later Academi).

The Big Corporation would take over the humblest of soldierly roles—the peeling of potatoes, the cooking of meals, the building of bases and outposts, the delivery of mail—and it would take up the gun (and the bomb), as well. Soon enough, even the dying would be outsourced to corporate hirees. Occupied Iraq and Afghanistan would be flooded with tens of thousands of private contractors and hired guns, while military men trained in elite special operations units would find big paydays by joining mercenary corporations doing similar work, often in the same war zones.

It was a remarkable racket. War and profit had long been connected in complicated ways, but seldom quite so straightforwardly. Now, win or lose on the battlefield, there would always be winners among the growing class of warrior corporations.

The AVF, pliant as a military should be, and backed by Madison Avenue to the tune of hundreds of millions of dollars to ensure that its ranks were full, would become ever more detached from most of American society. It would, in fact, become ever more foreign (as in "foreign legion") and ever more mercenary (as in the Hessians). The intelligence services of the national security state would similarly outsource significant parts of their work to the private sector. According to Dana Priest and William Arkin of the *Washington Post*, by 2010, about 265,000 of the 854,000 people with top security clearances were private contractors and "close to 30 percent of the workforce in the intelligence agencies [was] contractors."

No one seemed to notice, but a "1 percent" version of American war was coming to fruition, unchecked by a draft army, a skeptical Congress, or a democratic citizenry. In fact, Americans, generally preoccupied with lives in which our wars played next to no part, paid little attention.

Our Robot Military

Although early drone technology was already being used over North Vietnam, it's in another sense entirely that drones have been heading into America's future since 1973. There was an eerie logic to it: first came professional war, then privatized war, then mercenary and outsourced war— all of which made war ever more remote from most Americans. Finally, both literally and figuratively, came remote war itself.

It couldn't be more appropriate that the US Air Force prefers you not call their latest wonder weapons "unmanned aerial vehicles," or UAVs, anymore. They would like you to use the label "remotely piloted aircraft" (RPA) instead. And ever more remotely piloted that vehicle is to become, until—claim believers and enthusiasts—it will pilot itself, land itself, maneuver itself, and while in the air even choose its own targets.

In this sense, think of us as moving from the citizens' army to a roboticized, and finally robot, military—a foreign legion in the most basic sense. In other words, we are moving toward an ever greater outsourcing of war to things that cannot protest, cannot vote with their feet (or wings), and for whom there is no "home front" or even a home at all. In a sense, we are, as we have been since 1973, heading for a form of war without anyone, citizen or otherwise, in the picture—except those on the ground, enemy and civilian alike, who will, as usual, die.

Of course, it may never happen this way, in part because drones are anything but perfect or wonder weapons, and in part because corporate war fought by a thoroughly professional military turns out to be staggeringly expensive to the demobilized citizen, profligate in its waste, and—by the evidence of recent history—remarkably unsuccessful. It also couldn't be more remote from the idea of a democracy or a republic.

In a sense, the modern imperial age began hundreds of years ago with corporate war, when the Dutch, British, and other East India companies set sail, armed to the teeth, to subdue the world at a profit. Perhaps corporate war will also prove the endpoint for that age, the perfect formula for the last global empire on its way down.

A Cult of Government Secrecy

For us to gain a reasonable picture of our national security state, five, ten, twenty Snowdens, each at a different agency or outfit, would have to step out of the shadows—and that would just be for starters. Then we would need a media that was ready to roll and a Congress not wrapped in "security" and "secrecy" but demanding answers, as the Church Committee did in the Watergate era, with subpoenas in hand and the threat of prison for no-shows and perjurers.

Yes, we may have access to basic information about what the NSA has been up to, but what exactly do you know about the doings of the Pentagon's DIA, which has in recent years embarked on "an ambitious plan to assemble an espionage network that rivals the CIA in size"? How about the National Geospatial-Intelligence Agency, with its control over our system of spy satellites eternally prowling the planetary skies?

The answer is no more than you would have known about the NSA if Snowden hadn't acted as he did. And by the way, what do you really know about the FBI, which now, among other things, issues thousands of National Security Letters a year (16,511 in 2011 alone), an unknown number of them for terror investigations? Since their recipients are muzzled from discussing them, we know next to nothing about them or what the Bureau is actually doing. And how's your info on the CIA, which takes $4 billion more out of the intelligence "black budget" than the NSA, runs its own private wars, and has even organized its own privatized corps of spies as part of the general expansion of US intelligence and espionage abroad? The answer to all of the above is: remarkably little.

Or take something basic like that old-fashioned, low-tech form of surveillance: government informers and agents provocateurs. They were commonplace in the 1960s and early 1970s within every oppositional movement. Decades later, they are with us again. Thanks to the ACLU, which has mapped nationwide scattered reports on situations in which informers made it into at least the local news, we know that they infiltrated the antiwar movements that existed in these years, slipped into various aspects of the Occupy movement, and have run riot in local Muslim-American communities. We know as well that these informers come from a wide range of outfits, including the local police, the military, and the FBI. However, compared to what we know about NSA snooping and surveillance, we have almost no inside information on the extent of old-style informing, surveilling, and provoking.

One thing couldn't be clearer, though: the mania for secrecy has grown tremendously in the Obama years. On entering the Oval Office in 2009, Obama proclaimed a sunshine administration dedicated to "openness" and "transparency." That announcement now drips with irony. If you want a measure of the kind of secrecy the national security state considers proper and the White House condones these days, consider a *Los Angeles Times* article on the CIA's drone assassination program (one of the more overt aspects of Washington's covert world). The *Times* reported that chairman of the Senate Armed Services Committee Carl Levin held a "joint classified hearing" with the Senate Intelligence Committee on the CIA, the Pentagon, and their drone campaigns against terror suspects in the backlands of the planet. There was just one catch: CIA officials normally testify before only the House and Senate intelligence committees. In this case, the White House "refused to provide the necessary security clearances for members of the House and Senate armed services committees." As a result, it would not let CIA witnesses appear before Levin. Officials, reported the *Times*, "had little appetite for briefing the 26 senators and 62 House members who sit on the armed services committees on the CIA's most sensitive operations." Sunshine, in other words, is considered potentially dangerous, even in tiny doses, even in Congress.

In evaluating what may lurk behind Washington's many curtains, history does offer us a small hand. Thanks to the revelations of the 1970s, including a Snowden-style break-in by antiwar activists at an FBI office in Media, Pennsylvania, in 1971 that opened a window into the Bureau's acts of illegality, some now-famous reporting, and the thorough work of the Church Committee in the Senate, we have a sense of the enormity of what the US national security state was capable of when enveloped in a penumbra of secrecy. In the Johnson and Nixon years, as we now know, the FBI, the CIA, and the NSA committed a staggering range of misdeeds and crimes.

It's tempting to say that post-Watergate "reforms" made such acts a thing of the past. Unfortunately, there's no reason to believe this. In fact, the nature of that era's reforms should be reconsidered. After all, one particularly important congressional response of that moment was to create the FISA court, essentially a judiciary for the secret world, which would end up generating a significant body of law that no American outside the national security state could see.

The irony is overwhelming. After the shocking headlines, the congressional inquiries, the impeachment proceedings, the ending of two presidencies—one by resignation—and everything else, including black-bag jobs, break-ins, buggings, attempted beatings, blackmail, massive spying and surveillance, and provocations of every sort, the answer was a secret court. Its judges, appointed by the chief justice of the Supreme

Court alone, are charged with ruling after hearing only one side of any case involving a governmental desire to snoop or pry. Unsurprisingly enough, over the three and a half decades of its existence, the court has provided a willing rubber stamp for just about any urge of the national security state.

In retrospect, this remedy for widespread government illegality clearly was just another step in the institutionalization of a secret world that looks increasingly like an Orwellian nightmare. In creating the FISA court, Congress functionally took the seat-of-the-pants, extraconstitutional, extralegal acts of president Richard Nixon and put them under the rule of (secret) law.

Today, in the wake of the rampant extralegality of the Global War on Terror—including the setting up of a secret, extrajudicial global prison system of "black sites" where rampant torture and abuse were carried to the point of death, illegal kidnappings of terror suspects and their rendition to the prisons of torture regimes, and the assassination by drone of American citizens backed by Justice Department legalisms—it's clear that national security state officials feel they have near total impunity when it comes to whatever they want to do. They know that nothing they do, however egregious, will be brought before an open court of law and prosecuted. While the rest of us remain inside the legal system, they exist in what I've come to call post-legal America.

If tomorrow a series of Edward Snowdens were to appear, each from a different intelligence agency, one thing would be guaranteed: the shock of the NSA revelations would be multiplied many times over. Protected from the law by a spreading cult of government secrecy, beyond the reach of the citizenry, Congress, or the aboveground judicial system, supported by the White House and a body of developing secret law, knowing that no act undertaken in the name of American "safety" and "security" will ever be prosecuted, the inhabitants of our secret state have been moving in dark and disturbing ways. What we know is already disturbing enough. What we don't know would surely unnerve us far more.

A shadow government has conquered twenty-first-century Washington. We have the makings of a thug state of the first order.

Knowledge Is Crime

The members of the national security state, unlike the rest of us, exist in post-legal America. They know that, no matter how heinous the crime, they will not be brought to justice for it. The list of potentially serious criminal acts for which no one has had to take responsibility in a court of law is long, and has never, to my knowledge, been tabulated in one place. Here, then, is an initial rundown on seven of the most obvious crimes and misdemeanors of this era, for which no one has been held accountable.

- *Kidnapping*: After 9/11, the CIA got into kidnapping in a big way. At least 136 "terror suspects" and possibly many more (including completely innocent people) were kidnapped off the streets of global cities, as well as from the backlands of the planet, often with the help of local police or intelligence agencies. Fifty-four other countries were enlisted in the enterprise. The prisoners were delivered either into the Bush administration's secret global system of prisons, known as "black sites," to be detained and mistreated, or they were "rendered" directly into the hands of torture regimes from Egypt to Uzbekistan. No American involved has been brought to court for such illegal acts (nor did the US government ever offer an apology, no less restitution to anyone it kidnapped). One set of CIA agents was, however, indicted in Italy for a kidnapping and rendition to Egypt. Among them was the Agency's Milan station chief, Robert Seldon Lady. He had achieved brief notoriety for overseeing a *la dolce vita* version of rendition and later fled the country for the United States. Last year, he was briefly taken into custody in Panama, only to be spirited out of that country and back to safety by the US government.

- *Torture*: Similarly, it will be no news to anyone that, in their infamous "torture memos," officials of the Bush Justice Department freed CIA interrogators to "take the gloves off" and use what were euphemistically called "enhanced interrogation techniques" against offshore prisoners in the Global War on Terror. These included waterboarding, once known as "the water torture," and long defined even in this country as a form of torture. On coming to office, President Obama rejected these practices but refused to prosecute those who practiced them. Not a single CIA agent or private contractor involved was ever charged, no less brought to trial, nor was anyone in the Bush Justice Department or the rest of an administration that green-lighted these practices and whose top officials reportedly saw them demonstrated in the White House.

To be accurate, a single member of the national security state has gone to prison thanks to the CIA's torture program. That was John Kiriakou, a former CIA agent who tortured no one but offended the Obama administration by turning whistleblower and going public about torture by the CIA. He is now serving a thirty-month prison sentence "for disclosing a covert operative's name to a reporter." In other words, the only crime that could be prosecuted in connection with the agency's torture campaign was one that threatened to let the American public know more about it.

Now, however, thanks to leaks from the embattled Senate Intelligence Committee's 6,300-page report on the CIA's interrogation and torture program, we know that the Agency "used interrogation methods that weren't approved by the Justice Department or CIA headquarters." In other words, its agents went beyond even those techniques approved in the torture memos, which means that they acted illegally even by the dismal standards of the Bush administration. This should be an obvious signal for the beginning of prosecutions, but—not surprisingly—it looks like the only prosecution on the horizon might be of whoever leaked parts of the unreleased Senate report to McClatchy News.

- *Destroying evidence of a crime*: To purposely destroy evidence in order to impede a future investigation of possible criminal acts is itself, of course, a crime. We know that such a thing did indeed happen. Jose Rodriguez, Jr., the head of CIA clandestine operations, destroyed ninety-two videotapes of the repeated waterboarding of Khalid Sheikh Mohammed, who planned the 9/11 attacks, and alleged al-Qaeda operative Abu Zubaydah, "tapes that he had been explicitly told to preserve as part of an official investigation." The Justice Department investigated his act but never charged him. He has since defended himself in the book *Hard Measures*, saying that he was, in essence, "tired of waiting for Washington's bureaucracy to make a decision that protected American lives." He is still free and writing op-eds for the *Washington Post* praising the interrogation program whose tapes he destroyed.

- *Planning an extralegal prison system*: As is now well known, a global network of extralegal prisons, or "black sites," at which acts of torture and abuse of every sort could be committed was set up at the wishes of the highest officials of the Bush administration. This system was created specifically to avoid putting terror suspects into the US legal system. By definition, this was extralegal, if not illegal. It represented a concerted effort to avoid any of the constraints or oversight that US law or its courts might have imposed on the treatment of detainees. This was a well-planned crime committed not under the rubric of war against any specific power but of a global war without end against al-Qaeda and like-minded groups.

- *Killing detainees in that extralegal system*: The deaths of detainees in CIA custody in offshore (or borrowed) prisons as a result of harsh treatment ordered by their Agency handlers were not considered crimes. In two cases—in the "Salt Pit" in Afghanistan and at Abu Ghraib prison in Iraq—such deaths were investigated by the Justice Department, but no one was ever charged. In the case of Gul Rahman, the prisoner killed in the Salt Pit, according to the *Washington Post*, "[A] CIA officer allegedly ordered Afghan guards in November 2002 to strip Rahman and chain him to the concrete floor of his cell. Temperatures plunged overnight, and Rahman froze to death. Hypothermia was listed as the cause of death and Rahman was buried in an unmarked grave." (In a rare case brought before a military court, a low-level army interrogator was convicted of "killing an Iraqi general by stuffing him face-first into a sleeping bag," and sentenced to "forfeit $6,000 of his salary over the next four months, receive a formal reprimand, and spend 60 days restricted to his home, office, and church.")

- *Assassination*: Once upon a time, off-the-books assassination was generally a rare act of state and always one that presidents could deny. Now, it is part of everyday life in the White House and at the CIA. The president's role as assassin in chief has been all but publicly promoted as a political plus. The drone assassination campaigns in Pakistan, Yemen, and Somalia, though "covert" and run by a civilian agency (with much secret help from the US Air Force) are openly reported on in the media and discussed as a seeming point of pride by those involved. In 2009, for instance, then CIA director Leon Panetta didn't hesitate to enthusiastically praise the drone attacks in Pakistan as "the only game in town." And best of all, they are "legal." We know this because the White House had the Justice Department prepare a fifty-page document on their legality that it has refused to release to the public. In these campaigns in the backlands of distant places where there are seldom reporters, we nonetheless know that thousands of people have died, including significant numbers of children. Being run by a civilian agency, these cannot in any normal sense be "acts of war." In another world, they would certainly be considered illegal and possibly war crimes, as Christof Heyns, the UN special rapporteur on extrajudicial, summary, or arbitrary executions, has suggested. Top officials have taken responsibility for these acts, including the drone killings in Pakistan and Yemen of four American citizens condemned to death by a White House that has enthusiastically taken on the role of judge, jury, and executioner. No one involved, however, will ever see a day in court.

- *Perjury before Congress*: Lying to Congress in public testimony is, of course, perjury. Among others, we know that director of national intelligence James Clapper committed it in a strikingly bald-faced way on March 12, 2013. When asked by Senator Ron Wyden whether the NSA had gathered "any type of data at all on millions or hundreds of millions of Americans"—a question submitted to him a day in advance—Clapper answered, "No, sir. Not wittingly. There are cases where they could inadvertently perhaps collect, but not wittingly." This was a lie, pure and simple, as the Snowden revelations on the NSA's gathering of phone metadata on all Americans (including, we can reasonably deduce, our congressional representatives) would later make clear. Clapper subsequently apologized in a way that—were crime on anyone's mind—would essentially have been a confession. Congress did nothing, and Clapper remains the director of national intelligence with the "support" of the president.

Mind you, the above seven categories don't even take into account the sort of warrantless surveillance of Americans that should have put someone in a court of law, or the ways in which various warrior corporations overbilled or cheated the government in its war zones, or the ways private contractors "ran wild" in those same zones. Even relatively low-level crimes by minor figures in the national security state have normally not been criminalized. Take, for example, the private surveillance of and cyberstalking of "love interests," or "LOVEINT," by NSA employees using government surveillance systems. The NSA claims that at least one employee was "disciplined" for this, but no one was taken to court. A rare exception: a number of low-level military figures in the Abu Ghraib scandal were tried for their abusive actions, convicted, and sent to jail, though no one higher than a colonel was held accountable in court for those infamously systematic and organized acts of torture and abuse.

All in all, as with the banks after the meltdown of 2007–2008, even the most obvious of national security state crimes seem to fall into a "too big to fail" category. Call it "too big to jail." The only crime that repeatedly makes it out of the investigative phase and into court—as with State Department intelligence analyst Stephen Kim, Army Private First Class Chelsea Manning, and John Kiriakou—is revealing information the national security state holds dear. On that, the Obama administration has been fierce and prosecutorial.

If this weren't Washington 2014, but rather George Orwell's novel *1984*, then the sign emblazoned on the front of the Ministry of Truth—"WAR IS PEACE, FREEDOM IS SLAVERY, IGNORANCE IS STRENGTH"—would have to be amended to add a fourth slogan: KNOWLEDGE IS CRIME, or perhaps even KNOWLEDGE IS THE ONLY CRIME.

SIX

Why Washington Can't Stop

It stretched from the Caspian to the Baltic Sea, from the middle of Europe to the Kurile Islands in the Pacific, from Siberia to Central Asia. Its nuclear arsenal held forty-five thousand warheads, and its military had five million troops under arms. There had been nothing like it in Eurasia since the Mongols conquered China, took parts of Central Asia and the Iranian plateau, and rode into the Middle East, looting Baghdad. Yet when the Soviet Union collapsed in December 1991, by far the poorer, weaker imperial power disappeared.

And then there was one. There had never been such a moment: a single nation astride the globe without a competitor in sight. There wasn't even a name for such a state (or state of mind). "Superpower" had already been used when there were two. "Hyperpower" was tried briefly but didn't stick. "Sole superpower" stood in for a while but didn't satisfy. "Great Power," once the zenith of appellations, was by then a lesser phrase, left over from the centuries when various European nations and Japan were expanding their empires. Some started speaking about a "unipolar" world in which all roads led . . . well, to Washington.

To this day, we've never quite taken in that moment when Soviet imperial rot unexpectedly—above all, to Washington—became imperial crash-and-burn. Left standing, the Cold War's victor seemed, then, like an empire of everything under the sun. It was as if humanity had always been traveling toward this spot. It seemed like the end of the line.

After the rise and fall of the Assyrians and the Romans, the Persians, the Chinese, the Mongols, the Spanish, the Portuguese, the Dutch, the French, the English, the Germans, and the Japanese, some process seemed over. The United States was dominant in a previously unimaginable way—except in Hollywood films where villains cackled about their evil plans to dominate the world.

As a start, the United States was an empire of global capital. With the fall of Soviet-style communism (and the transformation of a Communist regime in China into a crew of authoritarian "capitalist roaders"), there was no other model for how to do anything, economically speaking. There was Washington's way—and that of the International Monetary Fund and the World Bank (both controlled by Washington)—or there was the highway, and the Soviet Union had already made it all too clear where that led: to obsolescence and ruin.

In addition, the United States had unprecedented military power. By the time the Soviet Union began to totter, America's leaders had for nearly a decade been consciously using "the arms race" to spend its opponent into an early grave. And here was the curious thing after centuries of arms races: when there was no one left to race, the United States continued an arms race of one.

In the years that followed, it would outpace all other countries or combinations of countries in military spending by staggering amounts. It housed the world's most powerful weapons makers, was technologically light years ahead of any other state, and was continuing to develop future weaponry for 2020, 2040, 2060, even as it established a near monopoly on the global arms trade (and so control over who would be well-armed and who wouldn't).

It had an empire of bases abroad, more than a thousand of them spanning the globe, also an unprecedented phenomenon. And it was culturally dominant, again in a way that made comparisons with other moments ludicrous. Like American weapons makers producing things that went boom in the night for an international audience, Hollywood's action and fantasy films took the world by storm. From blockbuster movies to the golden arches, the swoosh, and the personal computer, there was no other culture that could come close to claiming such a global cachet.

The key non-US economic powerhouses of the moment—Europe and Japan—maintained militaries dependent on Washington, had US bases littering their territories, and continued to nestle under Washington's "nuclear umbrella." No wonder that, in the United States, the post-Soviet moment was soon proclaimed "the end of history," and the victory of "liberal democracy" or "freedom" was celebrated as if there really were no tomorrow, only more of today.

Now jump into the new century and, decades after the Soviet Union disappeared, what's remarkable is how much—and how little—has changed.

On the how-much front: Washington's dreams of military glory ran aground with remarkable speed in Afghanistan and Iraq. Then, in 2007, the transcendent empire of capital came close to imploding as well, as a unipolar financial disaster spread across the planet. It led people to begin to wonder whether the globe's greatest power might not, in fact, be too big to fail, and we were suddenly—so everyone said—plunged into a "multipolar world."

Meanwhile, the Greater Middle East descended into protest, rebellion, civil war, and chaos without a Pax Americana in sight, as a Washington-controlled Cold War system in the region shuddered without (yet) fully collapsing. Washington's ability to impose its will on the planet looks ever more like the wildest of fantasies, while every sign, including the hemorrhaging of national treasure into losing trillion-dollar wars, reflects not ascendancy but possible decline.

And yet, in the how-little category: the Europeans and Japanese remain nestled under that American "umbrella," their territories still filled with US military bases. In the Eurozone, governments have continued to cut back on their investments in both NATO and their own militaries. Russia remains a country with a sizeable nuclear arsenal and a reduced but still significant military. Other regional powers—Turkey and Brazil, to name two—challenge US unipolarity economically but not militarily.

And then, of course, there is China. On the planet that humanity has inhabited these last several thousand years, can there be any question that China would have been the obvious pick to challenge, sooner or later, the dominion of the reigning great power of the moment? Estimates are that it will surpass the United States as the globe's number-one economy by perhaps 2030. Right now, the Obama administration seems to be working on just that assumption. With its well-publicized "pivot" to Asia (or "rebalancing"), it has been moving to "contain" what it fears might be the next great power. However, while the Chinese are indeed expanding their military and challenging their neighbors in the waters of the Pacific, there is no sign that the country's leadership is ready to embark on anything like a global challenge to the United States or that it could do so in any conceivable future. Its domestic problems, from pollution to unrest, remain burdensome enough that it's hard to imagine a China not absorbed with domestic issues through 2030 and beyond.

Militarily, culturally, and even to some extent economically, then, the United States remains surprisingly alone on Planet Earth in imperial terms, even if little has gone as planned in Washington. The story of the years since the Soviet Union fell may prove to be a tale of how American domination and decline went hand in hand, with the decline part of the equation being strikingly self-generated.

And yet here's a genuine, even confounding, possibility: that moment of "unipolarity" in the 1990s may really have been the endpoint of history as human beings had known it for millennia—the history, that is, of the rise and fall of empires. Could the United States actually be the last empire? Is it possible that there will be no successor because something has profoundly changed in the realm of empire building? One thing is increasingly clear: whatever the state of imperial America, something significantly more crucial to the fate of humanity (and of empires) is in decline. I'm talking, of course, about the planet itself.

The present capitalist model (the only one available, we are told) for a rising power, whether China, India, or Brazil, is also a model for planetary decline, possibly of a precipitous nature. The very definition of success—more middle-class consumers, more car owners, more shoppers, which means more energy used, more fossil fuels burned, more greenhouse gases entering the atmosphere—is also, as it never would have been before, the definition of failure. The greater the "success," the more intense the droughts, the stronger the storms, the more extreme the weather, the higher the rise in sea levels, the hotter the temperatures, the greater the chaos in low-lying or tropical lands, the more profound the failure. The question is: Will this put an end to the previous patterns of history, including the until-now-predictable rise of the next great power, the next empire? On a devolving planet, is it even possible to imagine the next stage in imperial gigantism?

Every factor that would normally lead toward "greatness" now also leads toward global decline. This process—which couldn't be more unfair to countries having their industrial and consumer revolutions late—gives a new meaning to Naomi Klein's term "disaster capitalism."

Take the Chinese, whose leaders, on leaving the Maoist model behind, did the most natural thing in the world at the time: they patterned their future economy on the United States—on, that is, success as it was then defined. Despite both traditional and revolutionary communal traditions, for instance, they decided that to be a power in the world, you needed to make the car (which meant the individual driver) a pillar of any future state-capitalist China. If it worked for the United States, it would work for them, and in the short run, it worked like a dream, a capitalist miracle—and China rose.

It was, however, also a formula for massive pollution, environmental degradation, and the pouring of ever more fossil fuels into the atmosphere in record amounts. And it's not just China. It doesn't matter whether you're talking about that country's ravenous energy use, including its possible future "carbon bombs," or the potential for US decline to be halted by new extreme methods of producing energy (fracking, tar-sands extraction, deep-water drilling). Such methods, however much they hurt local environments, might indeed turn the United States into a "new Saudi Arabia." Yet that, in turn, would only contribute further to the degradation of the planet, to decline on an ever-larger scale.

What if, in the twenty-first century, rising means declining? What if the unipolar moment turns out to be a planetary moment in which previously distinct imperial events—the rise and fall of empires—fuse into a single disastrous system?

Offshore Everywhere

We are entering a new world of military planning. Fewer troops, fewer full-frontal missions, no full-scale invasions, no more counterinsurgency.

That's the order of the day. Sure, American mega-bases, essentially well-fortified American towns plunked down in a strange land, including "embassies" the size of lordly citadels, aren't going away soon. After all, in base terms, we're already hunkered down in the Greater Middle East in an impressive way. And Washington has typically signaled in recent years that it's ready to fight to the last Japanese prime minister not to lose a single base among the three dozen it has on the Japanese island of Okinawa.

But here's the thing: even if the US military is dragging its old habits, weaponry, and global-basing ideas behind it, it's still heading offshore. There will be no more land wars on the Eurasian continent. Instead, greater emphasis will be placed on the navy, the air force, special operations forces, and a policy "pivot" to face China in southern Asia and a growing jihadist threat in Africa—both places where the American military position can be strengthened without more giant bases or monster embassies.

For Washington, "offshore" means the world's boundary-less waters and skies, but also, metaphorically, it means being repositioned off the coast of national sovereignty and all its knotty problems. This change, on its way for years, will officially rebrand the planet as a US free-fire zone, unchaining Washington from the limits that national borders once imposed. New ways to cross borders and new technology for doing it without permission are clearly in the planning stages, and US forces are being reconfigured accordingly.

The raid that killed Osama bin Laden is a harbinger of and model for what's to come. It was an operation cloaked in secrecy. There was no consultation with the "ally" on whose territory the raid was to occur. It involved combat by an elite special operations unit backed by drones and other high-tech weaponry and supported by the CIA. A national boundary was crossed with neither permission nor declaration of hostilities.

All the elements of this emerging formula for retaining planetary dominance have received plenty of publicity, but the degree to which they combine to assault traditional concepts of national sovereignty has been given little attention.

Since November 2002, when a Hellfire missile from a CIA-operated Predator drone turned a car with six alleged al-Qaeda operatives in Yemen into ash, such aircraft have led the way in this border-crossing, airspace-penetrating assault. The United States now has drone bases across the planet. Increasingly, the long-range reach of its drone program means that its planes can penetrate just about any nation's airspace. It matters little whether that country houses them itself. Take Pakistan, which in 2011 forced the CIA to remove its drones from Shamsi Air Base. Nonetheless, CIA drone strikes in that country's tribal borderlands continue, assumedly from bases in Afghanistan, and President Obama has offered a full-throated public defense of them.

Drones themselves are distinctly fallible, crash-prone machines. Still, they are, relatively speaking, cheap to produce. They can fly long distances across almost any border with no danger whatsoever to their human pilots and are capable of staying aloft for extended periods of time. They allow for surveillance and strikes anywhere. By their nature, they are border-busting creatures.

And keep in mind that when drones are capable of taking off from and landing on aircraft carrier decks, they will quite literally be offshore with respect to all borders but capable of crossing any. The navy's latest plans include a future drone that will land itself on those decks without a human pilot at any controls.

War has always been a quintessentially human and yet inhuman activity. Now, it seems, its inhuman aspect is on the rise. With the US military working to roboticize the future battlefield, the American way of war is destined to be imbued with *Terminator*-style terror.

Already American drones regularly cross borders in Pakistan, Somalia, and Yemen. Because of a drone downed in Iran, we know that they have also been flying surveillance missions in that country's airspace as—per the State Department—they are in Iraq and across parts of Africa. Washington is undoubtedly planning for far more of the same.

American War Enters the Shadows

Along with those skies filled with increasing numbers of drones goes a rise in US special operations forces. They, too, are almost by definition boundary-busting outfits. Once upon a time, an American president had his own "private army"—the CIA. Now, in a sense, he has his own private military. Formerly modest-sized units of elite special operations forces have grown into a force of sixty thousand, a secret military cocooned inside the larger military, and slated for further expansion and a larger budget. According to Nick Turse, in 2013 special operations units were deployed in 134 nations, more than two-thirds of the countries on earth.

By their nature, special operations forces work in the shadows: as hunter-killer teams, night raiders, and border-crossers. They function in close conjunction with drones and, as the regular army slowly withdraws from its giant garrisons in places like Europe, they are preparing to operate in a new world of stripped-down bases called "lily pads"—think frogs jumping across a pond to get their prey. No longer will the Pentagon be building American towns with all the amenities of home, but forward-deployed, minimalist outposts near likely global hotspots, like Camp Lemonnier in the North African nation of Djibouti.

Increasingly, American war itself will enter those shadows, where crossings of every sort of border, domestic as well as foreign, are likely to take place with little accountability to anyone except the president and the national security complex.

In those shadows, our secret forces are already melding into one another. A striking sign of this was the 2011 appointment as CIA director of a general who, in Iraq and Afghanistan, had relied heavily on special forces hunter-killer teams and night raiders, as well as drones, to do the job. Undoubtedly the most highly praised general of our American moment (before an affair gone awry forced him to resign in November 2012), General David Petraeus himself slipped into the shadows, where for more than a year he presided over covert civilian forces working ever more regularly in tandem with special operations teams and sharing drone assignments with the military.

And don't forget the navy, which couldn't be more offshore to begin with. It already operates eleven aircraft carrier task forces. These are, effectively, major American bases—massively armed small American towns—at sea. To these, the navy is adding smaller "bases." It has, for instance, retrofitted an old amphibious transport docking ship and sent it to the Persian Gulf either as a Navy SEAL commando "mother ship" or (depending on which Pentagon spokesperson you listen to) as a "lily pad" for countermine Sikorsky MH-53 helicopters and patrol craft. Whichever it is, it will just be a stopgap until the navy can build new "Afloat Forward Staging Bases" from scratch.

Futuristic weaponry now in the planning stages could add to the military's border-crossing capabilities. Take the army's Advanced Hypersonic Weapon or DARPA's Falcon Hypersonic Technology Vehicle 2, both of which are intended, someday, to hit targets anywhere on earth with massive conventional explosives in less than an hour.

From lily pads to aircraft carriers, advanced drones to special operations teams, it's offshore and into the shadows for US military policy. While the United States is economically in decline, it remains the sole military superpower on the planet. No other country pours anywhere near as much money into its military and its national security establishment or is likely to do so in the foreseeable future. It's clear enough that Washington is hoping to offset any economic decline with newly reconfigured military might. As in the old TV show, the United States has gun, will travel.

Onshore, American power in the twenty-first century has proved a disaster. Offshore, with Washington in control of the global seas and skies, with its ability to kick down the world's doors and strike just about anywhere without a by-your-leave or thank-you-ma'am, it hopes for better. As the early attempts to put this program into operation have indicated, however, be careful what you wish for: it sometimes comes home to bite you.

Washington's Unchecked Power

In terms of pure projectable power, there's never been anything like it. Its military has divided the world—the whole planet—into six "commands." Its fleet rules the seas and has done so largely unchallenged for almost seven decades. Its air force controls the global skies, and despite being almost continuously in action for years, hasn't faced an enemy plane since 1991 or been seriously challenged anywhere since the early 1970s. Its fleet of drone aircraft has proven itself capable of targeting and killing suspected enemies from Afghanistan and Pakistan to Yemen and Somalia with little regard for national boundaries. It funds and trains proxy armies on several continents and has complex aid and training relationships with militaries across the planet. On hundreds of bases, some tiny and others the size of American towns, its soldiers garrison the globe, with outposts from Honduras to Australia and on islands from Okinawa in the Pacific Ocean to Diego Garcia in the Indian Ocean. Its weapons makers are the most advanced on earth and dominate the global arms market. Its nuclear weaponry in silos, on bombers, and on its fleet of submarines would be capable of destroying several planets the size of Earth. Its system of spy satellites is unsurpassed and unchallenged. Its intelligence services can listen in on the phone calls or read the emails of almost anyone in the world, from top foreign leaders to obscure insurgents. The CIA and its expanding paramilitary forces are capable of kidnapping people of interest just about anywhere, from rural Macedonia to the streets of Rome and Tripoli. For its many prisoners, it has set up (and dismantled) secret jails across the planet and on its naval vessels. It spends more on its military than the next most powerful thirteen states combined. Add in the spending for its full national security state and it towers over any conceivable group of other nations.

In terms of advanced and unchallenged military power, there has been nothing like the US Armed Forces. No wonder American presidents now regularly use phrases like "the finest fighting force the world has ever known" to describe it. By the logic of the situation, the planet should be a pushover. Lesser nations with far lesser forces have controlled vast territories in the past. And despite much discussion of American decline and the waning of its power in a "multipolar" world, its ability to pulverize and destroy, kill and maim, blow up and kick down has only grown in this new century.

No other nation's military comes within a country mile. None has more than a handful of foreign bases. None has more than two aircraft carrier battle groups. No potential enemy has such a fleet of robotic planes. None has more than sixty thousand special operations forces. Country by country, it's no contest. The Russian (once "Red") Army is a shadow of its former self. The Europeans have not rearmed significantly. Japan's "self-defense" forces are powerful and slowly growing, but under the US nuclear "umbrella." Although China, regularly identified as the next rising imperial state, is involved in a much-ballyhooed military buildup, with its one aircraft carrier (a retread from the days of the Soviet Union), it remains only a regional power.

Despite this stunning global power imbalance, for more than a decade we have been given a lesson in what a military, no matter how overwhelming, can and (mostly) can't do on the twenty-first-century version of Planet Earth.

A Destabilization Machine

Let's start with what the United States can do. On this, the recent record is clear: it can destroy and destabilize. In fact, wherever US military power has been applied in recent years, if there has been any lasting effect at all, it has been to destabilize whole regions.

Back in 2004, almost a year and a half after American troops had rolled into a Baghdad looted and in flames, Amr Mussa, the head of the Arab League, commented ominously, "The gates of hell are open in Iraq." Although for the Bush administration the situation in that country was already devolving, to the extent that anyone paid attention to Mussa's description, it seemed over the top, even outrageous, as applied to American-occupied Iraq. Today, with the latest scientific estimate of Iraqi deaths caused by the invasion and war at 461,000, with thousands more a year still dying there, and with Syria in flames, it seems something of an understatement.

It's now clear that George W. Bush and his top officials, fervent fundamentalists when it came to the power of US military to alter, control, and dominate the Greater Middle East (and possibly the planet), launched the radical transformation of the region. Their invasion of Iraq punched a hole through the heart of the Middle East, sparking a Sunni-Shiite civil war that has now spread catastrophically to Syria, taking more than 150,000 lives there. They helped turn the region into a churning sea of refugees, gave life and meaning to a previously nonexistent al-Qaeda in Iraq (and now a Syrian version of the same), left Iraq drifting in a sea of roadside bombs and suicide bombers, and like other countries in the region, threatened with the possibility of splitting apart.

And that's just a thumbnail sketch. It doesn't matter whether you're talking about destabilization in Afghanistan, where US troops have been on the ground going on thirteen years; Pakistan, where a CIA-run drone air campaign in its tribal borderlands has continued for years as the country has grown ever shakier and more violent; Yemen (ditto), as an outfit called al-Qaeda in the Arabian Peninsula has grown ever stronger;

or Somalia, where Washington repeatedly backed proxy armies and supported outside incursions while an already destabilized country came apart, and the influence of al-Shabab, an increasingly violent Islamic group, seeped across regional borders. The results have always been the same: destabilization.

Consider Libya, where, no longer enamored with boots-on-the-ground interventions, President Obama sent in the air force, the drones, and the Tomahawk missiles in 2011 in a bloodless intervention (unless, of course, you were on the ground) that helped topple Muammar Qaddafi, the local autocrat, and his secret-police-and-prisons regime, and launched a vigorous young democracy . . . oh, wait a moment, not quite. In fact, the result, which, unbelievably enough, came as a surprise to Washington, was an increasingly damaged country with a desperately weak central government, a territory controlled by a range of militias, some Islamic extremist in nature, an insurgency and war across the border in neighboring Mali (thanks to an influx of weaponry looted from Qaddafi's vast arsenals), a dead American ambassador, a country almost incapable of exporting its oil, and so on.

Libya was, in fact, so thoroughly destabilized, so lacking in central authority that Washington felt free in October 2013 to dispatch US special operations forces onto the streets of its capital in broad daylight in an operation to snatch up a long-sought terrorist suspect, an act which was as "successful" as the toppling of the Qaddafi regime and, in a similar manner, further destabilized a government that Washington still theoretically backed. (Almost immediately afterward, the prime minister found himself briefly kidnapped by a militia unit as part of what might have been a coup attempt.)

No matter how much the masters of war in Washington pile up military technology, pour money into the armed forces, and outpace the rest of the world, none of it adds up to a hill of beans when it comes to making the world act as they wish. Yes, in Iraq, to take an example, Saddam Hussein's regime was quickly "decapitated," thanks to an overwhelming display of power and muscle by the invading Americans. His state bureaucracy was dismantled, his army demobilized, an occupying authority established backed by foreign troops, soon ensconced on huge multibillion-dollar military bases meant to be garrisoned for generations, and a suitably "friendly" local government installed. But the Bush administration's dreams ended in the rubble created by a set of poorly armed minority insurgencies, terrorism, and a brutal ethnic/religious civil war. In the end, despite the fact that the Obama administration and the Pentagon were eager to keep US troops stationed there in some capacity, a relatively weak central government refused, and they departed, the last representatives of the greatest power on the planet slipping away in the dead of night. Left behind among the ruins of historic ziggurats were the "ghost towns" and stripped or looted US bases that were to be our monuments in Iraq.

Today, under even more extraordinary circumstances, a similar process seems to be playing itself out in Afghanistan. After more than a decade there, finding itself incapable of suppressing a minority insurgency, Washington is slowly withdrawing its combat troops but wants to leave behind perhaps ten thousand "trainers" for the Afghan military and some special operations forces to continue the hunt for al-Qaeda and other terror types.

At least the Iraqi government had a certain strength of its own and the country's oil wealth to back it up. If there is a government on earth that qualifies for the term "puppet," it should be the Afghan one of president Hamid Karzai. After all, at least 80 percent (possibly 90 percent) of that government's expenses are covered by the United States and its allies, and its security forces are considered incapable of carrying on the fight against the Taliban and other insurgent outfits without US support and aid. If Washington were to withdraw totally (including its financial support), it's hard to imagine that any successor to the Karzai government would last long.

How, then, to explain the fact that Karzai refused to sign a future bilateral security pact, long in the process of being hammered out? Instead, he denounced US actions in Afghanistan, claimed that he simply would not ink the agreement, and began bargaining with US officials as if he were the leader of the planet's other superpower. A frustrated Washington had to dispatch secretary of state John Kerry on a sudden mission to Kabul for some top-level, face-to-face negotiations. The result, a reported twenty-four-hour marathon of talks and meetings, was hailed as a success: problem(s) solved. Oops, all but one—the very same one on which the continued US military presence in Iraq stumbled—Washington's demand for legal immunity from local law for its troops. In the end, Kerry flew out without an assured agreement.

Whether the US military does or doesn't last a few more years in Afghanistan, the blunt fact is that the president of one of the poorest and weakest countries on the planet, himself relatively powerless, is essentially dictating terms to Washington—and who's to say that, in the end, as in Iraq, US troops won't be forced to leave there, as well?

Once again, military strength has not carried the day. Yet military power, advanced weaponry, force, and destruction as tools of policy, as ways to create a world in your own image or to your own taste, have worked plenty well in the past. Ask those Mongols, or the European imperial powers from Spain in the sixteenth century to Britain in the nineteenth century, which took their empires by force and successfully maintained them over long periods.

What planet are we now on? Why is it that military power, the mightiest imaginable, can't overcome, pacify, or simply destroy weak powers, less than impressive insurgency movements, or the ragged groups of peoples we label "terrorists"? Why is such military power no longer transformative or even reasonably effective? Is it, to reach for an analogy, like antibiotics? If used for too long in too many situations, does a kind of immunity build up against it?

Let's be clear here: such a military remains a powerful potential instrument of destruction, death, and destabilization. For all we know—though it's not something we've seen anything of in recent years—it might also be a powerful instrument for genuine defense. But if recent history is any guide, what it clearly cannot be in the twenty-first century is a policy-making instrument, a means of altering the world to fit a scheme developed in Washington. The planet itself and people just about anywhere on it seem increasingly resistant in ways that take the military off the table as an effective superpower instrument of state.

Washington's military plans and tactics since 9/11 have been a spectacular train wreck. When you look back, counterinsurgency doctrine, resuscitated from the ashes of America's defeat in Vietnam, is once again on the scrap heap of history. Who today even remembers its key organizing phrase—"clear, hold, and build"—which now looks like the punch line for some malign joke? "Surges," once hailed as brilliant military strategy, have already disappeared into the mists. "Nation-building," once a term of tradecraft in Washington, is in the doghouse. "Boots on the ground," of which the United States had enormous numbers, are now a no-no. The American public is, everyone universally agrees, "exhausted" with war. Major American armies arriving to fight anywhere on the Eurasian continent in the foreseeable future? Don't count on it.

But lessons learned from the collapse of war policy? Don't count on that, either. It's clear enough that Washington still can't fully absorb what's happened. Its faith in war remains remarkably unbroken. Our leaders are still high on the counterterrorism wars of the future, even as they drown in their military efforts of the present.

Now the message is: skip those boots en masse—in fact, cut down on their numbers—and go for the counterterrorism package. No more spilling of (American) blood. Get the "bad guys," one or a few at a time, using the president's private army, the special operations forces, or his private air force, the CIA's drones. Build new bare-bones microbases globally. Move those aircraft carrier battle groups off the coast of whatever country you want to intimidate. Let local proxy forces with US trainers do the fighting for you.

It's clear we're entering a new period in terms of American war-making—the era of tiny wars, or microconflicts, especially in the tribal backlands of the planet.

So something is indeed changing in response to military failure, but what's not changing is Washington's preference for war as the option of choice, often of first resort. What's not changing is the thought that, if you can just get your strategy and tactics readjusted correctly, force will work.

What our leaders don't get is the most basic, practical fact of our moment: war simply doesn't work, not big, not micro. A superpower at war in the distant reaches of this planet is no longer a superpower ascendant but one with problems.

The US military may be a destabilization machine. It may be a blowback machine. What it's not is a policy-making or enforcement machine.

How a Thug State Operates

In 2011, the entire US government reportedly classified 92 million documents. If accurate and reasonably typical, that means, in the twenty-first century, the national security state has already generated more than a billion documents that could not be read by an American without a security clearance. Of those, thanks to one man, Edward Snowden, via various journalists, we have had access to a tiny percentage of perhaps 1.7 million of them. Or put another way, you, the voter, the taxpayer, the citizen—in what we still like to think of as a democracy—are automatically excluded from knowing or learning about most of what the national security state does in your name. That's unless, of course, its officials decide to selectively cherry-pick information they feel you are capable of safely and securely absorbing, or another Snowden releases documents to the world over the bitter protests, death threats, and teeth-gnashing of Washington officialdom and retired versions of the same.

So far, even among critics, the debate about what to make of Snowden's act has generally focused on "balance"; that is, on the right equilibrium between an obvious governmental need for secrecy and the security of the country, and an American urge for privacy, freedom, and transparency—for knowing, among other things, what your government is actually doing. Such a framework ("a meaningful balance between privacy and security") has proven a relatively comfortable one for Washington, which doesn't mind focusing on the supposedly knotty question of how to define the "limits" of secrecy and whistleblowing and what "reforms" are needed to bring the two into line. In the present context, however, such a debate seems laughable, if not absurd.

After all, it's clear from the numbers alone that the urge to envelop the national security state in a blanket of secrecy, to shield its workings from the eyes of its citizens (as well as allies and enemies) has proven essentially boundless, as have the secret ambitions of those running that state. There is no way, at present, to limit the governmental urge for secrecy even in minimal ways, certainly not via secret courts or congressional committees implicated and entangled in the processes of a secret system.

In the face of such boundlessness, perhaps the words *whistleblower* and *leaker*—both traditionally referring to bounded and focused activities—are no longer useful. Though we may not yet have a word to describe what Chelsea Manning, Julian Assange, and Edward Snowden have done, we should probably stop calling them whistleblowers. Perhaps they should instead be considered the creations of an overweening national security state, summoned by us from its id (so to speak) to act as a counterforce to its ambitions. Imagine them as representing our society's unconscious. Only in this way can we explain the boundlessness of their acts. After all, such massive document appropriations are inconceivable without a secret state endlessly in the process of documenting its own darkness.

One thing is for certain, though no one thinks to say it: despite their staggering releases of insider information, when it comes to the true nature and extent of the NSS, we surely remain in the dark. In the feeling that, thanks to Manning and Snowden, we now grasp the depths of that secret state, its secret acts, and the secret documentation that goes with it, we are undoubtedly deluded. In a sense, valuable as they have been, Snowden's revelations have helped promote this delusion. In a way that hasn't happened since the Watergate era of the 1970s, they have given us the feeling that a curtain has finally, definitively been pulled back on the true nature of the Washington system. Behind that curtain, we have indeed glimpsed a global-surveillance-state-in-the-making of astounding scope, reach, and technological proficiency, whose ambitions (and successes), even when not always fully achieved, should take our breath away. And yet, while this is accurate enough, it leads us to believe that we now know a great deal about the secret world of Washington. We don't.

Even if we knew what was in all of those 1.7 million NSA documents, they are a drop in the bucket. As of now, we have the revelations of one (marginal) insider who stepped out of the shadows to tell us about part of what a single intelligence agency documented about its own activities. The resulting global debate, controversy, anger, and discussion, Snowden has said, represents "mission accomplished" for him. But the mission shouldn't be considered accomplished for the rest of us.

SEVEN

Overwrought Empire

When the revelations of NSA contractor Edward Snowden began to hit the news and we suddenly found ourselves knee-deep in stories about PRISM, XKeyscore, and other Big Brother-ish programs that make up the massive global surveillance network the NSA has been building, I sat down and reread George Orwell's novel *1984*. At a moment when Americans were growing uncomfortably aware of the way their government was staring at them and storing what they had previously imagined as their private data, I had a moment of feeling a soaring sense of my own originality. It lasted only until I read an essay by NSA expert James Bamford in which he mentioned, "Within days of Snowden's documents appearing in the *Guardian* and the *Washington Post* ... bookstores reported a sudden spike in the sales of George Orwell's classic dystopian novel *1984*. On Amazon.com, the book made the 'Movers & Shakers' list and skyrocketed 6,021 percent in a single day." Nonetheless, amid a jostling crowd of worried Americans, I did keep reading that novel and found it at least as touching, disturbing, and riveting as I had when I first came across it sometime before Kennedy went on TV in 1962 to tell us the world might end in a Russian-American conflagration. Even today, it's hard not to marvel at the vision of a man living at the beginning of the television age who sensed how a whole society could be viewed, tracked, controlled, and surveilled.

But for all his foresight, Orwell had no more power to peer into the future than the rest of us. So it's no fault of his that, almost three decades after his year of choice, more than six decades after his death, the shape of our world has played havoc with his vision. Like so many others in his time and after, he couldn't imagine the disappearance of the Soviet Union or at least of Soviet-like totalitarian states. More than anything else, he couldn't imagine one fact of our world that, in 1948, wasn't in the human playbook.

In *1984*, Orwell imagined a future from what he knew of the Soviet and American (as well as Nazi, Japanese, and British) imperial systems. In conjuring up three equally balanced, equally baleful superpowers—Oceania, Eurasia, and Eastasia—balanced for an eternity in an unwinnable global struggle, he played out a logical extension of what had been developing on this planet for hundreds of years. His future was a version of the world humanity had lived with since the first European power mounted cannons on a wooden ship and set sail, like so many Mongols of the sea, to assault and conquer foreign realms, coastlines first. From that moment on, the imperial powers of this planet—super, great, prospectively great, and near great—came in contending or warring pairs, if not triplets or quadruplets. Portugal, Spain, and Holland; England, France, and Imperial Russia; the United States, Germany, Japan, and Italy (as well as Great Britain and France); and, after World War II, the United States and the Soviet Union.

Five centuries in which one thing had never occurred, the thing that even George Orwell, with his prodigious political imagination, couldn't conceive of, the thing that makes *1984* a dated work and his future a past that never was: a one-superpower world. To give birth to such a creature on such a planet—as indeed occurred in 1991—was to be at the end of history, at least as it had long been known.

Only in Hollywood fantasies about evil super-enemies was "world domination" by a single power imaginable. No wonder that, more than two decades into our one-superpower present, we still find it hard to take in this new reality and what it means.

At least two aspects of such a world seem, however, to be coming into focus. The evidence of the last decades suggests that the ability of even the greatest of imperial powers to shape global events may always have been somewhat exaggerated. The reason: power itself may never have been as centrally located in imperial or national entities as was once imagined. Certainly, with all rivals removed, the frustration of Washington at its inability to control events in the Greater Middle East and elsewhere could hardly be more evident. Still, Washington has proven incapable of grasping the idea that there might be forms of power, and so of resistance to American desires, not embodied in competitive states.

Evidence also seems to indicate that the leaders of a superpower, when not countered by another major power, when lacking an arms race to run or territory and influence to contest, may be particularly susceptible to the growth of delusional thinking, and in particular to fantasies of omnipotence.

Though Great Britain far outstripped any competitor or potential enemy at the height of its imperial glory, as did the United States at the height of the Cold War (the Soviet Union was always a junior superpower), there were at least rivals around to keep the leading power "honest" in its thinking. From December 1991, when the Soviet Union declared itself no more, there were none and, despite the dubious assumption by many in Washington that a rising China will someday be a major competitor, there remain none. Even if economic power has become more "multipolar," no actual state contests the American role on the planet in a serious way.

Just as still water is a breeding ground for mosquitoes, so single-superpowerdom seems to be a breeding ground for delusion. This is a phenomenon about which we have to be cautious, since we know little enough about it and are, of course, in its midst. But, so far, there seem to have been three stages to the development of whatever delusional process is under way.

Stage one stretched from December 1991 through September 10, 2001. Think of it as the decade of the stunned superpower. After all, the collapse of the Soviet Union went unpredicted in Washington and when it happened, the George H. W. Bush administration seemed almost incapable of processing it. In the years that followed, there was the equivalent of a stunned silence in the corridors of power.

After a brief flurry of debate about a post–Cold War "peace dividend," that subject dropped into the void, while, for example, US nuclear forces, lacking their major enemy of the previous several decades, remained more or less in place, strategically disoriented but ready for action. In those years, Washington launched modest and halting discussions of the dangers of "rogue states" (think "Axis of Evil" in the post-9/11 era), but the US military had a hard time finding a suitable enemy other than its former ally in the Persian Gulf, Iraq's Saddam Hussein. Its ventures into the world of war in Somalia and the former Yugoslavia were modest and not exactly greeted with rounds of patriotic fervor at home. Even the brief glow of popularity the elder Bush gained from his 1990–91 war against Iraq evaporated so quickly that, by the time he geared up for his reelection campaign barely a year later, it was gone.

In the shadows, however, a government-to-be was forming under the guise of a think tank. It was filled with figures, including future vice president Dick Cheney, future secretary of defense Donald Rumsfeld, future deputy secretary of defense Paul Wolfowitz, future UN ambassador John Bolton, and future ambassador to Afghanistan Zalmay Khalilzad, who firmly believed that the United States, with its staggering military advantage and lack of enemies, had an unparalleled opportunity to control and reorganize the planet. In January 2001, they came to power under the presidency of George W. Bush, eager for the opportunity to turn the United States into the kind of global dominator that would put the British and even Roman empires to shame.

Stage two in the march into single-superpower delusion began on September 11, 2001, only five hours after hijacked American Airlines Flight 77 smashed into the Pentagon. It was then that secretary of defense Donald Rumsfeld, already convinced that al-Qaeda was behind the attacks, nonetheless began dreaming about completing the First Gulf War by taking out Saddam Hussein. Of Iraq, he instructed an aide to "go massive . . . Sweep it all up. Things related and not." And go massive he and his colleagues did, beginning the process that led to the March 2003 invasion of Iraq, itself considered only a precursor to transforming the Greater Middle East into an American protectorate. Within days of the toppling of those towers in lower Manhattan, the Bush administration was already talking about launching a "war on terror," soon to become the "Global War on Terror." And they meant that "global." They were planning, in the phrase of the moment, to "drain the swamp"—everywhere.

In the early Bush years, dreams of domination bred like rabbits in single-superpower Washington. Such grandiose thinking quickly invaded administration and Pentagon planning documents as the Bush administration prepared to prevent potentially oppositional powers or blocs of powers from arising in the foreseeable future. No one, as its top officials and their neocon supporters saw it, could stand in the way of their planetary Pax Americana.

Nor, as they invaded Afghanistan, did they have any doubt that they would soon take down Iraq. It was all going to be so easy. Such an invasion, as one supporter wrote in the *Washington Post*, would be a "cakewalk." By the time American troops entered Iraq, the Pentagon already had plans on the drawing board to build a series of permanent bases—they preferred to call them "enduring camps"—and garrison that assumedly grateful country at the center of the planet's oil lands for generations to come.

Nobody in Washington was thinking about the possibility that an American invasion might create chaos in Iraq and surrounding lands. They assumed that Iran and Syria would be forced to bend their national knees to American power or that we would simply impose submission on them. (As a neoconservative quip of the moment had it, "Everyone wants to go to Baghdad. Real men want to go to Tehran.") And that, of course, would only be the beginning. Soon enough, no one would challenge American power. Nowhere. Never.

Such soaring dreams of—quite literally—world domination met no significant opposition in mainstream Washington. After all, how could they fail? Who on earth could possibly oppose them or the US military? The answer seemed too obvious to need to be stated—not until, at least, their all-conquering armies bogged down in Iraq and Afghanistan and the greatest power on the planet faced the possibility of defeat at the hands of . . . well, whom?

Until things went sour in Iraq, theirs would be a vision of the Goliath tale in which David (or various ragtag Sunni, Shiite, and Pashtun versions of the same) didn't even have a walk-on role. All other Goliaths were gone and the thought that such a set of minor Davids might pose problems for the planet's giant was beyond imagining, despite what the previous century's history of decolonization and resistance might have taught them. Above all, the idea that, at this juncture in history, power might not be located overwhelmingly and decisively in the most obvious place—in, that is, "the finest fighting force that the world has ever known"—seemed illogical in the extreme. Who in the Washington of that moment could have imagined that other kinds of power might, like so much dark matter in the universe, be mysteriously distributed elsewhere on the planet? Such was their sense of American omnipotence, such was the level of delusional thinking inside the Washington bubble.

Despite two treasury-draining disasters in Afghanistan and Iraq that should have been sobering when it came to the hidden sources of global power, especially the power to resist American wishes, such thinking showed only minimal signs of diminishing even as the Bush administration pulled back from Iraq, and a few years later, after a set of misbegotten "surges," the Obama administration decided to contemplate the same in Afghanistan.

Instead, Washington entered stage three of delusional life in a single-superpower world. Its main symptom: the belief in the possibility of controlling the planet not just through staggering military might but also through informational and surveillance omniscience and omnipotence. In these years, the urge to declare a global war on communications, create a force capable of launching wars in cyberspace, and storm the e-beaches of the Internet and the global information system proved overwhelming. The idea was to make it impossible for anyone to communicate or, in fact, do much of anything to which Washington might not be privy.

For most Americans, the Edward Snowden revelations would pull back the curtain on the way the NSA, in particular, has been building a global network for surveillance of a kind never before imagined, not even by the totalitarian regimes of the previous century. From domestic phone calls to international emails, from the bugging of UN headquarters and the European Union to eighty embassies around the world, from enemies to frenemies to allies, the system was remarkably all-encompassing. It had, in fact, the same aura of grandiosity about it, of overblown self-regard, that went with the launching of the Global War on Terror—the feeling that if Washington did it or built it, they would come.

I have no idea what the equivalents of the Afghan and Iraq wars will be in the surveillance world, but continue to build such a global system, ignoring the anger of allies and enemies alike, and "they" indeed will come. Such delusional grandiosity cannot help but generate resistance and blowback in a perfectly real world that, whatever Washington thinks, maintains a grasp on perfectly real power, even without another imperial state on any horizon.

Today, the US position in the world seems even more singular. American military bases still dot the planet in remarkable profusion at a moment when no other nation on earth has more than a handful outside its territory. The reach of Washington's surveillance and intelligence networks is unique in the history of the planet. This should be the dream formula for a world dominator and yet no one can look at Planet Earth today and not see that the single superpower is limited indeed in its ability to control developments. Its president couldn't even form a "coalition of the willing" to launch a limited series of missile attacks on the military facilities of the Syrian regime of Bashar al-Assad. From Latin America to the Greater Middle East, the American system is visibly weakening, while at home, inequality and poverty are on the rise, infrastructure crumbles, and national politics is in a state of permanent "gridlock."

Such a world should be fantastical enough for the wildest sort of dystopian fiction, for perhaps a novel titled *2014*. What, after all, are we to make of a planet with a single superpower that lacks genuine enemies of any significance and that, to all appearances, has nonetheless been fighting a permanent global war with . . . well, itself—and appears to be losing?

Victory Culture

Americans lived in a "victory culture" for much of the twentieth century. You could say that we experienced an almost seventy-five-year stretch of triumphalism from World War I to the end of the Cold War, with time off for a destructive stalemate in Korea and a defeat in Vietnam too shocking to absorb or shake off. When the Soviet Union disintegrated in 1991, it all seemed so obvious. Fate had clearly dealt Washington a royal flush. It was victory with a capital V. The United States was, after all, the last standing superpower, with hardly a "rogue state" on the horizon. It was almost unnerving, such clear sailing into a dominant future, but a moment for the ages nonetheless. Within a decade, pundits in Washington were hailing us as "the dominant power in the world, more dominant than any since Rome."

And here's the odd thing: in a sense, little has changed since then— yet everything seems different. This is the American imperial paradox: everywhere there are now "threats" against our well-being that seem to demand action and yet nowhere are there commensurate enemies to go with them.

At one level, the American situation should simply take your breath away. Never before in modern history had there been an arms race of only one or a great power confrontation of only one. And at least in military terms, just as the neoconservatives imagined in those early years of the twenty-first century, the United States remains the "sole superpower" or even "hyperpower" on Planet Earth.

Yet the more dominant the US military becomes in its ability to destroy and the more its forces are spread across the globe, the more the defeats and semi-defeats pile up, the more the missteps and mistakes grow, the more the strains show, the more the suicides rise, the more the nation's treasure disappears down a black hole—and in response to all of this, the more moves the Pentagon makes.

A great power without a significant enemy? You might have to go back to the Roman Empire at its height or some Chinese dynasty in full flower to find anything like it. Osama bin Laden is dead. The original al-Qaeda is reportedly a shadow of its former self. The great regional threats of the moment, North Korea and Iran, are regimes held together by baling wire and the suffering of their populaces. The only incipient great power rival on the planet, China, has just launched its first aircraft carrier, a refurbished Ukrainian throwaway from the 1990s.

The US government is investing an estimated $1.45 trillion to produce and operate a single future aircraft, the F-35—more than any country, the United States included, now spends on its national defense annually. The US military is singular in other ways, too. It alone has divided the globe into six "commands." With (lest anything be left out) an additional command, Stratcom, for the heavens and another, recently established, for the only space not previously occupied, cyberspace, where we're already unofficially "at war." No other country on the planet thinks of itself in faintly comparable military terms.

When its high command plans for its future "needs," thanks to chairman of the joint chiefs of staff General Martin Dempsey, they repair (don't say "retreat") to a military base south of the capital where they argue out their future and war-game various possible crises while striding across a map of the world larger than a basketball court. What other military would come up with such a method?

The president now has at his command not one but two private armies, the CIA, and an expanding elite, the Joint Special Operations Command, members of whom are now deployed to hot spots around the globe. Across much of the global south, there is no sovereign space Washington's drones can't penetrate to kill those judged by the White House to be threats.

In sum, the United States is now the sole planetary Top Gun in a way that empire-builders once undoubtedly fantasized about, but that none from Genghis Khan to Adolf Hitler has ever achieved. In fact, by every measure (except success), the likes of it has never been seen.

By all the usual measuring sticks, the United States should be supreme in a historically unprecedented way. And yet it couldn't be more obvious that it's not, that despite all the bases, elite forces, private armies, drones, aircraft carriers, wars, conflicts, strikes, interventions, and clandestine operations, despite a labyrinthine intelligence bureaucracy that never seems to stop growing and into which we pour a minimum of close to $70 billion a year, nothing seems to work out in an imperially satisfying way. It couldn't be more obvious that this is not a glorious dream, but some kind of ever-expanding imperial nightmare.

US military power has been remarkably discredited globally by the most pitiful of forces. From Pakistan to Honduras, just about anywhere it goes in the old colonial or neocolonial world, known in the contested Cold War era as the Third World, resistance of one unexpected sort or another arises and failure ensues in some often long-drawn-out and spectacular fashion. Certainly, it's in some way related to the more than half-century of decolonization movements, rebellions, and insurgencies that were a feature of the previous century. It also has something to do with the way economic heft has spread beyond the United States, Europe, and Japan—with the rise of the "tigers" in Asia, the explosion of the Chinese and Indian economies, the advances of Brazil and Turkey, and the movement of the planet toward some kind of genuine economic multi-polarity. It may also have something to do with the end of the Cold War, which put an end as well to several centuries of imperial or great power competition and left the sole "victor," it now seems clear, heading toward the exits wreathed in self-congratulation.

It's as if the planet itself, or humanity, had somehow been inoculated against the imposition of imperial power, as if it now rejected it whenever and wherever applied. In the previous century, it took a half-nation, North Korea, backed by Russian supplies and Chinese troops to fight the United States to a draw, or a popular insurgent movement backed by a local power, North Vietnam, backed in turn by the Soviet Union and China to defeat American power. Now, small-scale minority insurgencies, largely using roadside bombs and suicide bombers, are fighting American power to a draw (or worse) with no great power behind them at all.

Washington's Wars on Autopilot

After the last decade of military failures, standoffs, and frustrations, you might think that this would be apparent in Washington. After all, the United States is now visibly an overextended empire, its sway waning from the Greater Middle East to Latin America, the limits of its power increasingly evident. And yet, here's the curious thing: two administrations in Washington have drawn none of the obvious conclusions. We are not just a classically overextended empire but also an overwrought one, operating on some kind of militarized autopilot. Lacking is a learning curve. By all evidence, it's not just that there isn't one, but that there can't be one.

Washington, it seems, now has only one mode of thought and action, no matter who is at the helm or what the problem may be, and it always involves, directly or indirectly, openly or clandestinely, the application of militarized force. Nor does it matter that each subsequent application only destabilizes some region yet more or undermines further what once were known as "American interests."

Take Libya, as an example. It briefly seemed to count as a rare American military success story: a decisive intervention in support of a rebellion against a brutal dictator—so brutal, in fact, that the CIA previously shipped "terrorist suspects," Islamic rebels fighting against the Qaddafi regime, there for torture. No US casualties resulted, while American and NATO air strikes were decisive in bringing a set of ill-armed, ill-organized rebels to power.

In the world of unintended consequences, however, the fall of Qaddafi sent Tuareg mercenaries from his militias, armed with high-end weaponry, across the border into Mali. There, when the dust settled, the whole northern part of the country had come unhinged and fallen under the sway of Islamic extremists and al-Qaeda wannabes as other parts of North Africa threatened to destabilize. At the same time, of course, the first American casualties of the intervention occurred when Ambassador Christopher Stevens and three other Americans died in an attack on the Benghazi consulate and a local "safe house."

With matters worsening regionally, the response from Washington couldn't have been more predictable. As Greg Miller and Craig Whitlock of the *Washington Post* reported in October 2012, the White House had begun planning for military operations against al-Qaeda in the Maghreb (North Africa), now armed with weaponry pillaged from Qaddafi's stockpiles. These plans evidently included the approach used in Yemen (US special forces on the ground and CIA drone strikes), or a Somalia "formula" (drone strikes, special forces operations, CIA operations, and the support of African proxy armies), or even at some point "the possibility of direct U.S. intervention."

In addition, Eric Schmitt and David Kilpatrick of the *New York Times* reported that the Obama administration was "preparing retaliation" against those it believes killed the US ambassador, possibly including "drone strikes, special operations raids like the one that killed Osama bin Laden, and joint missions with Libyan authorities." The near certainty that, like the previous intervention, this set of military actions would only further destabilize the region with yet more unpleasant surprises and unintended consequences hardly seemed to matter. Nor did the fact that, in crude form, the results of such acts are known to us ahead of time affect the unstoppable urge to plan and order them.

Such situations are increasingly legion across the Greater Middle East and elsewhere. Take one other tiny example: Iraq, from which, after almost a decade-long military disaster, the "last" US units essentially fled in the middle of the night as 2011 ended. Even in those last moments, the Obama administration and the Pentagon were still trying to keep significant numbers of US troops there (and, in fact, did manage to leave behind hundreds as trainers of elite Iraqi units). Iraq has been supportive of the embattled Syrian regime and drawn ever closer to Iran, even as its own sectarian strife has ratcheted upward. Having watched this unsettling fallout from its last round in the country, according to the *New York Times*, the United States was in September 2012 trying to negotiate an agreement "that could result in the return of small units of American soldiers to Iraq on training missions. At the request of the Iraqi government, according to [Lieutenant General Robert L.] Caslen, a unit of army special operations soldiers was recently deployed to Iraq to advise on counterterrorism and help with intelligence." The urge to return to the scene of their previous disaster was evidently unstaunchable.

You could offer various explanations for why our policymakers, military and civilian, continue in such a repetitive and—even from an imperial point of view—self-destructive vein in situations where unpleasant surprises are essentially guaranteed and lack of success a given. Yes, there is the military-industrial complex to be fed. Yes, we are interested in the control of crucial resources, especially energy, and so on. But it's probably more reasonable to say that a deeply militarized mindset and the global maneuvers that go with it are by now just part of the way of life of a Washington eternally "at war." They are the tics of a great power with the equivalent of Tourette's Syndrome. They happen because they can't help but happen, because they are engraved in the policy DNA of our national security complex, and can evidently no longer be altered. In other words, they can't help themselves.

That's the only logical conclusion in a world where it has become ever less imaginable to do the obvious, which is far less or nothing at all. Downsizing the mission? Inconceivable. Thinking the unthinkable? Don't even give it a thought!

America as a Shining Drone Upon a Hill

Here's the essence of it: you can trust America's crème de la crème, the most elevated, responsible people—no matter what weapons, what powers, you put in their hands. You needn't look over *their* shoulders. Yes, placed in the hands of evildoers, those weapons and powers could create a living nightmare. But controlled by the best of people, they lead to measured, thoughtful, precise decisions in which bad things are (with rare and understandable exceptions) done only to truly terrible types. In the process, you simply couldn't be better protected.

And in case you were wondering, there is no question who among us are the best, most lawful, moral, ethical, considerate, and judicious people: the officials of our national security state. Trust them.

You may be paying a fortune to maintain their world—the 30,000 people hired to listen in on conversations and other communications in this country, the 230,000 employees of the Department of Homeland Security, and beyond—but there's a good reason. That's what's needed to make truly elevated, surgically precise decisions about life and death in the service of protecting American interests on this dangerous globe of ours. And in case you wondered just how we know all this, we have it on the best authority: the people who are doing it—the only ones, given the obvious need for secrecy, capable of judging just how moral, elevated, and remarkable their own work is. They deserve our congratulations, but if we're too distracted to give it to them, they are quite capable of high-fiving themselves.

We're talking, in particular, about the use by the Obama administration, like the Bush administration before it, of a growing armada of remotely piloted planes, also known as drones, grimly labeled Predators and Reapers, to fight a nameless, almost planet-wide war. Its purpose: to destroy anyone else we believe might ever endanger our "interests." In the service of this war, in the midst of a perpetual state of war and of wartime, every act committed by these leaders is, it turns out, absolutely, totally, and completely legal. We have their say-so for that, and they have the documents to prove it, largely because the best and most elevated legal minds among them have produced that documentation in secret. Of course, they dare not show it to the rest of us, lest lives be endangered.

By their own account, they have, in fact, been covertly exceptional, moral, and legal for more than a decade (minus, of course, the odd black site and torture chamber)—so covertly exceptional, in fact, that they haven't quite gotten the credit they deserve. Now, they would like to make the latest version of their exceptional mission to the world known to the rest of us. It is finally in our interest, it seems, to be a good deal better informed about America's covert wars.

No one should be surprised. There was always an "overt" lurking in the "covert" of what now passes for "covert war." The CIA's global drone assassination campaign has long been a bragging point in Washington, even if it couldn't officially be discussed directly before, say, Congress. The covertness of our drone wars in the Pakistani tribal borderlands, Somalia, Yemen, and elsewhere turns out to have less to do with secrecy—just about every covert drone strike is reported, sooner or later, in the media—than assuring two administrations that they could pursue their drone wars without accountability to anyone.

In many ways, these days, American exceptionalism is about as unexceptional as apple pie. It has, for one thing, become the everyday language of the campaign trail. And that shouldn't surprise us either. After all, great powers and their leaders tend to think well of themselves. The French had their *mission civilisatrice*, the Chinese had the "mandate of heaven," and like all imperial powers they inevitably thought they were doing the best for themselves and others in this best of all possible worlds.

Sometimes, though, the American version of this self-regard does seem surreal. If you want to get a taste of just what this means, consider a speech John Brennan, then the president's counterterrorism "tsar," gave in April 2012 at the Woodrow Wilson International Center for Scholars. According to his own account, he was dispatched to the center by President Obama to provide greater openness when it came to the administration's secret drone wars, to respond to critics of the drones and their legality, and undoubtedly to put a smiley face on drone operations generally.

Ever since the Puritan minister John Winthrop first used the phrase in a shipboard sermon on the way to North America, "a city upon a hill" has captured something of at least one American-style dream—a sense that this country's fate was to be a blessed paragon for the rest of the world, an exception to every norm. In the last century, the phrase became "a shining city upon a hill" and was regularly cited in presidential addresses. Whatever that "city," that dream, was once imagined to be, it has undergone a largely unnoticed metamorphosis in the twenty-first century. It has become—even in our dreams—an up-armored garrison encampment, just as Washington itself has become the heavily fortified bureaucratic heartland of a war state. So when Brennan spoke, what he offered was a new version of American exceptionalism: the first "shining drone upon a hill" speech.

Never, according to him, has a country with such an advanced weapon system as the drone used it quite so judiciously, quite so—if not peacefully—at least with the sagacity and skill usually reserved for the gods. American drone strikes, he assured his listeners, are "ethical and just," "wise," and "surgically precise"—exactly what you'd expect from a country he refers to, quoting the president, as the preeminent "standard bearer in the conduct of war." Our drone strikes, he added, are based on staggeringly "rigorous standards" involving the individual identification of human targets. Even when visited on American citizens outside declared war zones, they are invariably "within the bounds of the law," as you would expect of the preeminent "nation of laws."

The strikes are never motivated by vengeance, always target someone known to us as the worst of the worst, and almost invariably avoid anyone who is even the most mediocre of the mediocre. Forget the fact that, as Greg Miller of the *Washington Post* reported, the CIA has received permission from the president to launch drone strikes in Yemen based only on the observed "patterns of suspicious behavior" of groups of unidentified individuals, as was already true in the Pakistani tribal borderlands.

Yes, in such circumstances innocents do unfortunately die, even if unbelievably rarely—and for that we couldn't be more regretful. Such deaths, however, are in some sense salutary, since they lead to the most rigorous reviews and reassessments of, and so improvements in, our actions. "This too," Brennan assured his audience, "is a reflection of our values as Americans."

"I would note," he added, "that these standards, for identifying a target and avoiding . . . the loss of lives of innocent civilians, exceed what is required as a matter of international law on a typical battlefield. That's another example of the high standards to which we hold ourselves."

And that was just a taste of the tone and substance of the speech given by the president's leading counterterrorism expert of that moment, and in it he was no outlier. It caught something about an American sense of self. Yes, Americans might be ever more down on the Afghan war, but like their leaders, they are high on drones. In a *Washington Post*/ABC News poll, 83 percent of respondents supported the administration's use of drones. Perhaps that's not surprising either, since the drones are generally presented here as the coolest of machines, as well as cheap alternatives (in money and lives) to sending more armies onto the Eurasian mainland.

Predator Nation

In recent years, the United States has pioneered the development of the most advanced killing machines on the planet. In the process, we have turned much of the rest of the planet into what can only be considered an American free-fire zone.

We have, in short, established a remarkably expansive set of drone-war rules for the global future. Naturally, we trust ourselves with such rules, but there is a fly in the ointment, even as the droniacs see it. Others far less sagacious, kindly, lawful, and good than we are do exist on this planet and they may soon have their own fleets of drones. At the time of Brennan's speech, about fifty countries were already buying or developing such robotic aircraft, including Russia, China, and Iran. And who knows what terror groups are looking into suicide drones?

As the *Washington Post*'s David Ignatius put it in a column about that speech: "What if the Chinese deployed drones to protect their workers in southern Sudan against rebels who have killed them in past attacks? What if Iran used them against Kurdish separatists they regard as terrorists? What if Russia used them over Chechnya? What position would the United States take, and wouldn't it be hypocritical if it opposed drone attacks by other nations that face 'imminent' or 'significant' threats?"

This is Washington's global drone conundrum as seen from inside the Beltway. These are the nightmarish scenarios even our leaders can imagine others producing with their own drones and our rules. A deeply embedded sense of American exceptionalism, a powerful belief in their own special, self-evident goodness, however, conveniently blinds them to what they are doing right now. Looking in the mirror, they are incapable of seeing a mask of death. And yet our proudest export at present may be a stone-cold robotic killer with a name straight out of a horror movie.

The "shining drones" launched on campaigns of assassination and slaughter are increasingly the "face" that we choose to present to the world, even as the president, with his "kill list" and his meetings to pick those who are to die, has quite literally become the country's assassin in chief. And yet it's beyond us why such a reality might not shine for others. In fact, what we increasingly look like to those others is a Predator nation. And not just to the parents and relatives of the more than 160 children the Bureau of Investigative Journalism has documented as having died in US drone strikes in Pakistan.

War is now the only game in town. As for peace, to the managers of our national security state, it's neither a word worth mentioning nor an imaginable condition. In truth, our leaders should be in mourning for whatever peaceful dreams we ever had. But mention drones and they light up. They're having a love affair with those machines. They just can't get enough of them or imagine their world or ours without them.

What they can't see in the haze of exceptional self-congratulation is this: they are transforming the promise of America into a promise of death. And death, visited from the skies, isn't precise. It isn't glorious. It isn't judicious. It certainly isn't a shining vision. It's hell. And it's a global future for which, someday, no one will thank us.

EIGHT

The Obama Contradiction

President Barack Obama has few constraints (except those he's internalized). No one can stop him or countermand his orders. He has a bevy of lawyers at his beck and call to explain the "legality" of his actions. And if he cares to, he can send a robot assassin to kill you, whoever you are, no matter where you may be on Planet Earth.

He sounds like a typical villain from a James Bond novel. You know, the kind who captures Bond, tells him his fiendish plan for dominating the planet, ties him up for some no less fiendish torture, and then leaves him behind to gum up the works.

As it happens, though, he's the president of the United States, a nice guy with a charismatic wife and two lovely kids.

How could this be?

Sometimes to understand where you are, you need to ransack the past. In this case, to grasp just how this country's first African-American-constitutional-law-professor-liberal Oval Office holder became the most imperial of all recent imperial presidents, it's necessary to look back to the early years of George W. Bush's presidency. Who today even remembers that time, when it was common to speak of the United States as the only "sheriff" on the planet?

In those first high-flying years after 9/11, President Bush, Vice President Cheney, and their top officials held three dreams of power and dominance that they planned to make reality. The first was to loose the US military on the Greater Middle East. The invasion of Iraq in 2003 was to be only the initial act in a series of a shock-and-awe operations in which Washington would unilaterally rearrange the oil heartlands of the planet. This, in turn, would position the United States to control the planet in a historically unique way, and so prevent the rise of any other great power or bloc of nations resistant to American desires.

Their second dream, linked at the hip to the first, was to create a gen-erations-long Pax Republicana at home. In that dream, the Democratic Party, like the Iraqis or the Iranians, would be brought to heel, a new Re-publican majority funded by corporate America would rule the roost, and above it all would be perched a "unitary executive," a president freed of domestic constraints and capable—by fiat, the signing statement, or simply expanded powers—of doing just about anything he wanted.

Though less than a decade has passed, both of those dreams already feel like ancient history. Both crashed and burned, leaving behind a De-mocrat in the White House, an Iraq without an American military gar-rison, and a still un-regime-changed Iran. With the arrival on Bush's watch of a global economic meltdown, those too-big-not-to-fail dreams were relabeled disasters, fed down the memory hole, and are today largely forgotten.

It's easy, then, to forget that the Bush era wasn't all crash-and-burn, that the third of their hubristic fantasies proved a remarkable, if barely noticed, success. Because that success never fully registered amid succes-sive disasters and defeats, it's been difficult for Americans to grasp, amid domestic gridlock, the "imperial" part of the Obama presidency.

Remember that Cheney and his cohorts took power in 2001 con-vinced that, post-Watergate, post-Vietnam, American presidents had been placed in "chains." As soon as 9/11 hit, they began, as they put it, to "take the gloves off." Their deepest urge was to use "national security" to free George W. Bush and his successors of any constraints. From this urge flowed the decision to launch a "Global War on Terror"—that is, to es-tablish a "wartime" with no possible end that would leave a commander-in-chief president in the White House till hell froze over. The construction of Guantánamo and the creation of "black sites" from Poland to Thailand—the president's own private offshore prison system—followed naturally, as did the creation of his own privately sanctioned form of (in)justice and punishment, a torture regime.

At the same time, they began expanding the realm of presidentially ordered "covert" military operations (most of which were, in the end, well publicized)—from drone wars to the deployment of special operations forces. These were signposts indicating the power of an unchained president to act without constraint abroad. Similarly, at home, the Bush administration began expanding what would once have been illegal surveillance of citizens and other forms of presidentially inspired overreach. They began, in other words, treating the United States as if it were part of an alien planet, as if it were, in some sense, a foreign country and they the occupying power.

With a cowed Congress and a fearful, distracted populace, they undoubtedly were free to do far more. There were few enough checks and balances left to constrain a war president and his top officials. It turned out, in fact, that the only real checks and balances were internalized ones, or those that came from within the national security state itself, and yet those evidently still limited what they felt was possible.

This, then, was what Barack Obama inherited on entering the Oval Office: an expanding, but not yet fully expansive, commander-in-chief presidency, which, in retrospect, seemed to fit him like a glove. Of course, he also inherited the Bush administration's domestic failures and those in the Greater Middle East, and they overshadowed what he's done with that commander-in-chief presidency.

It's true that, with president Harry Truman's decision to go to war in Korea in 1950, Congress's constitutional right to declare war (rather than rubber-stamp a presidential announcement of the same) went by the boards. So there's a distinct backstory to our present imperial presidency. Still, in our era, presidential war-making has become something like a 24/7 activity.

Once upon a time, American presidents didn't consider micromanaging a permanent war state as a central part of their job description, nor did they focus so unrelentingly on the US military and the doings of the national security state. Today, the president's word is death just about anywhere on the planet and he exercises that power with remarkable frequency. He appears in front of "the troops" increasingly often and his wife has made their well-being part of her duties. He has at his command expanded "covert" powers, including his own private armies: a more militarized CIA and growing hordes of special operations forces, who essentially make up a "covert" military inside the US military.

In effect, he also has his own private intelligence outfits, including most recently a newly formed Defense Clandestine Service at the Pentagon, focused on non–war zone intelligence operations (especially, so the reports go, against China and Iran). Finally, he has what is essentially his own expanding private (robotic) air force: drones. He can send his drone assassins and special ops troops just about anywhere to kill just about anyone he thinks should die, national sovereignty be damned. He firmly established his "right" to do this by going after the worst of the worst, killing Osama bin Laden in Pakistan with special operations forces and an American citizen and jihadi, Anwar al-Awlaki, in Yemen with a drone.

Before Obama ordered the successful drone assassination of Awlaki, lawyers from the Pentagon, State Department, National Security Council, intelligence agencies, and the Department of Justice Office of Legal Counsel held meetings to produce a fifty-page memorandum providing a "legal" basis for the president to order the assassination of a US citizen, a document, mind you, that will never be released to the public.

In truth, at this point the president could clearly have ordered those deaths without such a document. Think of it as the presidential equivalent of a guilty conscience, but when those drones start taking out people in Yemen and elsewhere based on nothing more than patterns of behavior, there will be no stream of fifty-page memorandums generated to cover the decisions. That's because as you proceed down such a path, as your acts become ever more the way of your world, your need to justify them (to yourself, if no one else) lessens.

That path, already widening into a road, may, someday, become the killing equivalent of an autobahn. In that case, making such decisions will be ever easier for an imperial president as American society grows yet more detached from the wars fought and operations launched in its name. In terms of the president's power to kill by decree, the reach of the commander-in-chief presidency and the "covert" campaigns, so secret they can't even be acknowledged in a court of law, so public they can be boasted about, will only increase.

This is a dangerous development, which leaves us in the grip—for now—of what might be called the Obama conundrum. On the one hand, at home, on issues of domestic importance, Obama is a hamstrung, hogtied president, strongly checked and balanced. Since the passage of his embattled healthcare bill, he has, in a sense, been in chains, able to accomplish next to nothing of his domestic program. Even when trying to exercise the unilateral powers that have increasingly been invested in presidents, what he can do on his own has proven exceedingly limited, a series of tiny gestures aimed at the largest of problems.

On the other hand, the power of the president as commander in chief has never been greater. If Obama is the president of next to nothing on the domestic policy front, he has the powers previously associated with the gods when it comes to war-making abroad. There, he is the purveyor of life and death. At home, he is a hamstrung weakling: at war he is—to use a term that has largely disappeared since the 1970s—an imperial president.

Praying at the Church of St. Drone: The President and His Apostles

The last two presidents may not have been emperors or kings, but they—and the vast national-security structure that continues to be built up and institutionalized around the presidential self—are certainly one of the nightmares the founding fathers of this country warned us against. They are one of the reasons those founders put significant war powers in the hands of Congress, which they knew would be a slow, recalcitrant, deliberative body.

Thanks to a long 2012 *New York Times* piece by Jo Becker and Scott Shane, "Secret 'Kill List' Proves a Test of Obama's Principles and Will," we now know that the president has spent startling amounts of time overseeing the "nomination" of terrorist suspects for assassination via the remotely piloted drone program he inherited from president George W. Bush, which he has expanded exponentially. Moreover, that article was based largely on interviews with "three dozen of his current and former advisers." In other words, it was essentially an administration-inspired piece—columnist Robert Scheer calls it "planted"—on a "secret" program the president and those closest to him are quite proud of and wanted to brag about in an election year.

The language of the piece about our warrior president was generally sympathetic, even in places soaring. It focused on the moral dilemmas of a man who has personally approved and overseen the growth of a remarkably robust assassination program in Yemen, Somalia, and Pakistan, based on a "kill list." Moreover, he's regularly done so target by target, name by name. According to Becker and Shane, President Obama has also been involved in the use of a fraudulent method of counting drone kills, one that unrealistically deemphasizes civilian deaths.

Historically speaking, this is all passing strange. The *Times* calls Obama's role in the drone killing machine "without precedent in presidential history." And that's accurate. It's not that American presidents have never had anything to do with or been in any way involved in assassination programs. The state as assassin is not new in our history. Consider, for example, the assassination plots against Cuba's Fidel Castro, the Congo's Patrice Lumumba, and South Vietnamese autocrat (and ostensible ally) Ngo Dinh Diem. (Lumumba and Diem were successfully murdered.) During Lyndon Johnson's presidency, the CIA carried out a massive assassination campaign in Vietnam, Operation Phoenix. It proved staggeringly profligate and was responsible for the deaths of tens of thousands of Vietnamese, both actual enemies and those simply swept up in the process.

In previous eras, however, presidents either stayed above the assassination fray or practiced a kind of plausible deniability about the acts. We are surely at a new stage in the history of the imperial presidency when an administration fosters a story that's meant to broadcast collective pride in the president as assassin in chief.

Religious Cult or Mafia Hit Squad?

Who now remembers that, in the early years of his presidency, George W. Bush kept what the *Washington Post*'s Bob Woodward called "his own personal scorecard for the war" on terror? It took the form of photographs with brief biographies and personality sketches of those judged to be the world's most dangerous terrorists, each ready to be crossed out by Bush once captured or killed. That scorecard was, Woodward added, always available in a desk drawer in the Oval Office.

Such private presidential recordkeeping now seems penny-ante indeed. The distance we've traveled in a decade can be measured by the *Times*'s description of the equivalent of that "personal scorecard" today (something no desk drawer could hold):

> It is the strangest of bureaucratic rituals: Every week or so, more than 100 members of the government's sprawling national security apparatus gather, by secure video teleconference, to pore over terrorist suspects' biographies and recommend to the president who should be the next to die. This secret "nominations" process is an invention of the Obama administration, a grim debating society that vets the Power-Point slides bearing the names, aliases, and life stories of suspected members of Al Qaeda's branch in Yemen or its allies in Somalia's Shabab militia. The nominations go to the White House, where by his own insistence and guided by [counterterrorism "tsar" John] Brennan, Mr. Obama must approve any name.

In other words, thanks to such meetings—on what insiders have labeled "terror Tuesday"—assassination has been thoroughly institutionalized, normalized, and bureaucratized around the figure of the president. Without the help of or any oversight from the American people or their elected representatives, he alone is now responsible for regular killings thousands of miles away, including those of civilians and even children. On that score, his power is total and completely unchecked. He can prescribe death for anyone "nominated," choosing any of the "baseball cards" (PowerPoint bios) on that kill list and then order the drones to take them, or others in the neighborhood, out. He and he alone can decide that assassinating known individuals isn't enough and that the CIA's drones can instead strike at suspicious "patterns of behavior" on the ground in Yemen or Pakistan. He can stop any attack, any killing, but there is no one, nor any mechanism, that can stop him. A US global killing machine (quite literally so, given that growing force of drones) is now at the beck and call of a single, unaccountable individual.

In the process, as Glenn Greenwald has pointed out, the president has shredded the Fifth Amendment, guaranteeing Americans that they will not "be deprived of life, liberty, or property, without due process of law." The Justice Department's Office of Legal Counsel produced a secret memo claiming that, while the Fifth Amendment's due process guarantee does apply to the drone assassination of an American citizen in a land with which we are not at war, "it could be satisfied by internal deliberations in the executive branch." (That, writes Greenwald, is "the most extremist government interpretation of the Bill of Rights I've heard in my lifetime.") In other words, the former constitutional law professor has been freed from the law of the land in cases in which he "nominates," as he has, US citizens for robotic death.

There is, however, another aspect to the institutionalizing of those "kill lists" and assassination as presidential prerogatives that has gone unmentioned. If the *Times* article—which largely reflects how the Obama administration cares to see itself and its actions—is to be believed, the drone program is also in the process of being sanctified and sacralized. You get a sense of this from the language of the piece itself. ("A parallel, more cloistered selection process at the C.I.A. focuses largely on Pakistan…") The president is presented as a particularly moral man, who devotes himself to the "just war" writings of religious figures like Thomas Aquinas and St. Augustine, and takes every death as his own moral burden. Brennan, who became Obama's leading counterterrorism advisor, was earlier in his career in the CIA knee-deep in the Bush-era torture controversy, but is presented, quite literally, as a priest of death, not once but twice in the piece. He is described by the *Times* reporters as "a priest whose blessing has become indispensable to Mr. Obama." They then quote the man who was then the State Department's top lawyer, Harold H. Koh, as saying, "It's as though you had a priest with extremely strong moral values who was suddenly charged with leading a war."

In the *Times* telling, the organization of robotic killing had become a kind of cult of death within the Oval Office, with those involved in it being so many religious devotees. We may be, that is, at the edge of a new state-directed, national security–based religion of killing grounded in the fact that we are in a dangerous world and the safety of Americans is our preeminent value. In other words, the president, his apostles, and his campaign acolytes are all, it seems, praying at the Church of St. Drone.

Thought about another way, "terror Tuesdays" evoke not so much a monastery or a church synod as a Mafia council directly out of a Mario Puzo novel, with the president as the Godfather, designating "hits" in a rough-and-tumble world.

How far we've come in just two presidencies. Assassination as a way of life has been institutionalized in the Oval Office—and thoroughly normalized.

After 5,719 inside-the-Beltway (largely inside-the-Oval-Office) words, the *Times* piece finally gets to this single outside-the-Beltway sentence: "Both Pakistan and Yemen are arguably less stable and more hostile to the United States than when Mr. Obama became president."

Arguably, indeed. For the few who read that far, it was a brief reminder of just how narrow, how confining the experience of worshipping at St. Drone actually is. All those endless meetings, all those presidential hours, and the two countries that have taken the brunt of the drone raids are more hostile, more dangerous, and in worse shape than in 2009. And one of them, keep in mind, is a nuclear power. News articles since have emphasized further how powerfully those drones have radicalized local populations—however many "bad guys" (and children) they may also have wiped off the face of the Earth.

And though the *Times* doesn't mention this, it's not just bad news for Yemen or Pakistan. American democracy, already on the ropes, is worse off, too.

What should astound Americans—but seldom seems to be noticed—is just how into the shadows, how thoroughly military-centric, and how unproductive has become Washington's thinking at the altar of St. Drone and its equivalents (including special operations forces). As we learned in the *Times* article, we not only have an assassin in chief in the Oval Office but also a cyberwarrior, perfectly willing to release a new form of weaponry, the most sophisticated computer "worm" ever developed, against another country with which we are not at war. This represents a breathtaking kind of rashness, especially from the leader of a country that, perhaps more than any other, is dependent on computer systems, opening the United States to potentially debilitating kinds of future blowback. Once again, as with drones, the White House is setting the global rules of the road for every country (and group) able to get its hands on such weaponry, and it's hit the highway at 140 miles per hour without a cop in sight.

James Madison, Thomas Jefferson, George Washington, and the rest of them knew war and yet were not acolytes of the eighteenth-century equivalents of St. Drone, or of presidents who might be left free to choose to turn the world into a killing zone. They knew at least as well as anyone in our national security state today that the world is always a dangerous place—and that that's no excuse for investing war powers in a single individual. They didn't think that a state of permanent war, a state of permanent killing, or a president free to plunge Americans into such states was a reasonable way for their new republic to go. To them, it was by far the more dangerous way to exist in our world.

The founding fathers would, I suspect, have chosen republican democracy over safety. They would never have believed that a politician surrounded by advisors and lawyers, left to his own devices, could protect them from what truly mattered. They tried to guard against it. Now, we have a government and a presidency dedicated to it, no matter whom we elect.

NINE

Destroying the Planet for Record Profits

We have a word for the conscious slaughter of a racial or ethnic group: *genocide*. And one for the conscious destruction of aspects of the environment: *ecocide*. But we don't have a word for the conscious act of destroying the planet we live on, the world as humanity had known it until, historically speaking, late last night. A possibility might be *terracide*, from the Latin word for Earth. It has the right ring, given its similarity to the commonplace danger word of our era: terrorist.

The truth is, whatever we call them, it's time to talk bluntly about the *terrarists* of our world. Yes, 9/11 was horrific. Almost three thousand dead, massive towers down, apocalyptic scenes. And yes, when it comes to terror attacks, the Boston Marathon bombings weren't pretty either. But in both cases, those who committed the acts paid for or will pay for their crimes.

In the case of the terrarists—and here I'm referring in particular to the men who run what may be the most profitable corporations on the planet, giant energy companies like ExxonMobil, Chevron, ConocoPhillips, BP, and Shell—you're the one who's going to pay, especially your children and grandchildren. You can take one thing for granted: not a single terrarist will ever go to jail, yet they certainly knew what they were doing.

It isn't that complicated. In recent years, the companies they run have been extracting fossil fuels from the earth in ever more frenetic and ingenious ways. The burning of those fossil fuels, in turn, has put record amounts of carbon dioxide (CO_2) into the atmosphere. In 2013, the CO_2 level reached four hundred parts per million for the first time in human history. A consensus of scientists has long concluded that the process was warming the world and that, if the average planetary temperature rose more than two degrees Celsius, all sorts of dangers could ensue, including seas rising high enough to inundate coastal cities, increasingly intense heat waves, droughts, floods, ever more extreme storm systems, and so on.

How to Make Staggering Amounts of Money and Do In the Planet

None of this is exactly a mystery. It's in the scientific literature. NASA scientist James Hansen first publicized the reality of global warming to Congress in 1988. It took a while—thanks in part to the terrarists—but the news of what was happening increasingly made it into the mainstream. Anybody could learn about it.

Those who run the giant energy corporations knew perfectly well what was going on and could, of course, have read about it in the papers like the rest of us. And what did they do? They put their money into funding think tanks, politicians, foundations, and activists intent on emphasizing "doubts" about the science (since it couldn't actually be refuted); they and their allies energetically promoted what came to be known as climate denialism. Then they sent their agents and lobbyists and money into the political system to ensure that their plundering ways would not be obstructed. And in the meantime, they redoubled their efforts to get ever "tougher" and sometimes "dirtier" energy out of the ground in ever tougher and dirtier ways.

The peak oil people hadn't been wrong when they suggested years ago that we would soon hit a limit in oil production from which decline would follow. The problem was that they were focused on traditional or "conventional" liquid oil reserves, obtained from large reservoirs in easy-to-reach locations on land or near shore. Since then, the big energy companies have invested a remarkable amount of time, money, and (if I can use that word) energy in the development of techniques that would allow them to recover previously unrecoverable reserves (sometimes by processes that themselves burn striking amounts of fossil fuels): fracking, deep-water drilling, and tar sands production, among others.

They also began to go after huge deposits of what energy expert Michael Klare calls "extreme" or "tough" energy—oil and natural gas that can only be acquired through the application of extreme force or that requires extensive chemical treatment to be usable as a fuel. In many cases, moreover, the supplies being acquired, like heavy oil and tar sands, are more carbon-rich than other fuels and emit more greenhouse gases when consumed. These companies have even begun using climate change itself—in the form of a melting Arctic—to exploit enormous and previously unreachable energy supplies. With the imprimatur of the Obama administration, Royal Dutch Shell, for example, has been preparing to test out possible drilling techniques in the treacherous waters off Alaska.

Call it irony, if you will, or call it a nightmare, but Big Oil evidently has no qualms about making its next set of profits directly off melting the planet. Its top executives continue to plan their futures, and so ours, knowing that their extremely profitable acts are destroying the very habitat, the very temperature range that for so long made life comfortable for humanity.

Their prior knowledge of the damage they are doing is what should make this a criminal activity. And there are corporate precedents for this, even if on a smaller scale. The lead paint industry, the asbestos industry, and the tobacco companies all knew the dangers of their products, made efforts to suppress the scientific information or instill doubt about it even as they promoted the glories of what they made, and went right on manufacturing and selling while others suffered and died.

And here's another similarity: with all three industries, the negative results conveniently arrived years, sometimes decades, after exposure and so were hard to connect to it. Each of these industries knew that the relationship existed. Each used that time disconnect as protection. One difference: if you were a tobacco, lead, or asbestos executive, you might be able to ensure that your children and grandchildren weren't exposed to your product. In the long run, that's not a choice when it comes to fossil fuels and CO_2, as we all live on the same planet (though it's also true that the well-off in the temperate zones are unlikely to be the first or worst to suffer).

If Osama bin Laden's 9/11 plane hijackings or the Tsarnaev brothers' homemade bombs at the Boston Marathon constitute terror attacks, why shouldn't what the energy companies are doing fall into a similar category (even if on a scale that leaves those events in the dust)? And if so, then where is the national security state when we really need it? Shouldn't its job be to safeguard us from terrarists and terracide, as well as terrorists and their destructive plots?

The Alternatives That Weren't

It didn't have to be this way.

On July 15, 1979, at a time when gas lines, sometimes blocks long, were a disturbing fixture of American life, president Jimmy Carter spoke directly to the American people on television for thirty-two minutes, calling for a concerted effort to end the country's oil dependence on the Middle East. "To give us energy security," he announced,

> I am asking for the most massive peacetime commitment of funds and resources in our nation's history to develop America's own alternative sources of fuel—from coal, from oil shale, from plant products for gasohol, from unconventional gas, from the sun . . . Just as a similar synthetic rubber corporation helped us win World War II, so will we mobilize American determination and ability to win the energy war. Moreover, I will soon submit legislation to Congress calling for the creation of this nation's first solar bank, which will help us achieve the crucial goal of 20 percent of our energy coming from solar power by the year 2000.

It's true that, at a time when the science of climate change was in its infancy, Carter's vision of "alternative energy" wasn't exactly a fossil fuel–free one. Even then—shades of today or possibly tomorrow—he was talking about having "more oil in our shale alone than several Saudi Arabias." Still, it was a remarkably forward-looking speech.

Had we invested massively in alternative energy research and development back then, who knows where we might be today? Instead, the media dubbed the "malaise speech," though the president never actually used that word, speaking instead of an American "crisis of confidence." While the initial public reaction seemed positive, it didn't last long. In the end, the president's energy proposals were essentially laughed out of the room and ignored for decades.

As a symbolic gesture, Carter had thirty-two solar panels installed on the White House and said: "A generation from now, this solar heater can either be a curiosity, a museum piece, an example of a road not taken, or it can be a small part of one of the greatest and most exciting adventures ever undertaken by the American people: harnessing the power of the sun to enrich our lives as we move away from our crippling dependence on foreign oil." As it turned out, "a road not taken" was the accurate description. On entering the Oval Office in 1981, Ronald Reagan caught the mood of the era perfectly. One of his first acts was to order the removal of those panels. None were reinstalled for three decades, until after Barack Obama became president.

Carter would, in fact, make his mark on US energy policy, just not quite in the way he had imagined. Six months later, on January 23, 1980, in his last State of the Union address, he would proclaim what came to be known as the Carter Doctrine: "Let our position be absolutely clear," he said. "An attempt by any outside force to gain control of the Persian Gulf region will be regarded as an assault on the vital interests of the United States of America, and such an assault will be repelled by any means necessary, including military force."

No one would laugh him out of the room for that. Instead, the Pentagon would fatefully begin organizing itself to protect US (and oil) interests in the Persian Gulf on a new scale and America's oil wars would follow soon enough. Not long after that address, it would start building up the Rapid Deployment Force in the Gulf, which would in time become the US Central Command. More than three decades later, ironies abound: thanks in part to those oil wars, whole swaths of the energy-rich Middle East are in crisis, if not chaos, while the big energy companies have put time and money into a staggeringly fossil fuel–heavy version of Carter's "alternative" North America. They've focused on shale oil, and on shale gas as well, and with new production methods, they are reputedly on the brink of turning the United States into a "new Saudi Arabia."

If true, this would be the worst, not the best, of news. In a world where what used to pass for good news increasingly guarantees a nightmarish future, energy "independence" of this sort means the extraction of ever more extreme energy, ever more CO$_2$ heading skyward, and ever more planetary damage in our collective future. This was not the only path available to us, or even to Big Oil. With their historic profits, the major oil companies could have decided anywhere along the line that the future they were ensuring was beyond dangerous. They could themselves have led the way with massive investments in genuine alternative energies (solar, wind, tidal, geothermal, algal, and who knows what else), instead of the exceedingly small-scale ones they made, often for publicity purposes. They could have backed a widespread effort to search for other ways that might, in the decades to come, have offered something close to the energy levels fossil fuels now give us. They could have worked to keep the extreme-energy reserves that turn out to be surprisingly commonplace deep in the Earth. And we might have had a different world—from which, by the way, they would undoubtedly have profited handsomely.

Instead, what we've got is the equivalent of a tobacco company situation, but on a planetary scale. To complete the analogy, imagine for a moment that they were planning to produce even more prodigious quantities not of fossil fuels but of cigarettes, knowing what damage they would do to our health. Then imagine that, without exception, everyone on earth was forced to smoke several packs of them a day. If that isn't a terrorist—or terrarist—attack of an almost unimaginable sort, what is? If the oil execs aren't terrarists, then who is? And if that doesn't make the big energy companies criminal enterprises, then how would you define that term?

To destroy our planet with malice aforethought, with only the most immediate profits on the brain, with only your own comfort and well-being (and those of your shareholders) in mind: Isn't that the ultimate crime?

Climate Change as the Antinews

When it comes to climate change—perhaps the great security threat humanity faces today—there is no "story," not in the normal news sense anyway. The fact that 97 percent of scientists who have weighed in on the issue believe that climate change is a human-caused phenomenon is not a story. That only 1 of 9,137 peer-reviewed papers on climate change published between November 2012 and December 2013 rejected human causation is not a story either, nor is the fact that only 24 out of 13,950 such articles did so over twenty-one years. That the anything-but-extreme Intergovernmental Panel on Climate Change (IPCC) offers an at least 95 percent guarantee of human causation for global warming is not a story, nor is the recent revelation that IPCC experts believe we only have fifteen years left to rein in carbon emissions or we'll need new technologies not yet in existence, which may never be effective. Nor is the recent poll showing that only 47 percent of Americans believe climate change is human-caused (a drop of 7 percent since 2012) or that the percentage who believe climate change is occurring for any reason has also declined since 2012 from 70 percent to 63 percent. Nor is the fact that, as the effects of climate change came ever closer to home, media coverage of the subject dropped between 2010 and 2012. Nor is it a story that European nations, already light-years ahead of the United States on phasing out fossil fuels, recently began considering cutbacks on some of their climate change goals, nor that US carbon emissions actually rose in 2013, nor that the southern part of the much disputed Keystone XL pipeline, which is to bring particularly carbon-dirty tar sands from Alberta, Canada, to the US Gulf Coast, is now in operation, nor that 2013 was either the fourth or seventh hottest year on record, depending on how you evaluate the numbers.

Don't misunderstand me. Each of the above was reported somewhere and climate change itself is an enormous story, if what you mean is Story with a capital S. It could even be considered the Story of all Stories. It's just that climate change and its component parts are unlike every other story, from the Syrian slaughter and the problems of Obamacare to New Jersey governor Chris Christie's Bridgegate or Justin Bieber's latest shenanigans. The future of all other stories, of the news and storytelling itself, rests on just how climate change manifests itself over the coming decades or even century. What happens in midterm or presidential elections, in our wars, politics, and culture, who is celebrated and who ignored—none of it will matter if climate change devastates the planet.

Climate change isn't the news and it isn't a set of news stories. It's the prospective end of all news. Think of it as the antinews.

All the rest is part of the prospective annals of human history: the rise and fall of empires, of movements, of dictatorships and democracies, of just about anything you want to mention. The most crucial stories, like the most faddish ones, are—every one of them—passing phenomena, which is of course what makes them the news.

Climate change isn't. New as that human-caused phenomenon may be—having its origins in the Industrial Revolution—it is nonetheless on a different scale than everything else, which is why journalists and environmentalists often have so much trouble figuring out how to write about it. While no one who, for instance, lived through "Frankenstorm" Sandy on the East Coast in 2012 could call the experience "boring"—winds roaring through urban canyons like freight trains, lights going out across lower Manhattan, subway tunnels flooding, a great financial capital brought to its proverbial knees—in news terms, much of global warming is boring and repetitive. I mean, drip, drip, drip. How many times can you write about the melting Arctic sea ice or shrinking glaciers and call it news? How often are you likely to put that in your headlines?

We're so used to the phrase "the news" that we often forget its essence: what's "new" multiplied by that "s." It's true that the "new" can be repetitively so. How many times have you seen essentially the same story about Republicans and Democrats fighting on Capitol Hill? But the momentousness of climate change, which isn't hard to discern, is difficult to regularly turn into meaningful "new" headlines ("Humanity Doomed If . . ."), to repeatedly and successfully translate into a form focused on the present and the passing moment, on what happened yesterday or today or might possibly happen tomorrow.

If the carbon emissions from fossil fuels are allowed to continue to accumulate in the atmosphere, the science of what will happen sooner or later is relatively clear, even if its exact timetable remains in question: this world will be destabilized, as will humanity, along with countless other species. We could, at the worst, essentially burn ourselves off Planet Earth. This would prove a passing event for the planet itself, but not for us, or for any fragment of humanity that managed to survive in some degraded form, or for the civilizations we've developed over thousands of years.

In other words, unlike "the news," climate change and its potential devastations exist on a time scale not congenial either to media time or to the individual lifetimes of our short-lived species. Great devastations and die-offs have happened before. Give the planet a few million years and life of many sorts will regenerate and undoubtedly thrive. But possibly not us.

Nuclear Dress Rehearsal

We went through a dress rehearsal for this moment in the twentieth century when dealing—or not dealing—with nuclear weapons, aka the Bomb (often capitalized in my youth as a sign of how nuclear disaster was felt to be looming over life itself). With the dropping of that "victory weapon" on two Japanese cities in August 1945, a new era opened. For the first time, we humans—initially in Washington, then in Moscow, then in other national capitals—took the power to end all life on this planet into our own hands. You could think of it as the single greatest, if also grimmest, act of secularization in history. From 1945 on, at least prospectively, we could do what only God had previously been imagined capable of: create an End Time on this planet.

In itself, that was a remarkable development. And there was nothing figurative about it. The US military was involved in what, in retrospect, can only be considered operational planning for world's end. In its first "Single Integrated Operational Plan," or SIOP, in 1960, for instance, it prepared to deliver more than 3,200 nuclear weapons to 1,060 targets in the Communist world, including at least 130 cities that would then, if all went well, cease to exist. Official estimates of casualties ran to 285 million dead and 40 million injured. (Those figures undoubtedly underestimated radiation and other effects, and today we know that the exploding of so many nuclear weapons would have ended life as we know it on this planet.) In those years, in the most secret councils of government, American officials also began to prepare for the possibility that 100 Russian missiles might someday land on US targets, killing or injuring 22 million Americans. Not so many years later, the weaponry of either of the superpowers had the capability of destroying the planet many times over.

The United States and the USSR were by then locked in a struggle that gained a remarkably appropriate acronym: MAD (for "mutually assured destruction"). During the Cold War, the United States built an estimated 70,000 nuclear warheads and bombs of every size and shape, the Soviet Union 55,000, and with them went a complex semisecret nuclear geography of missile silos, plutonium plants, and the like that shadowed the everyday landscape we knew.

In 1980, scientists discovered a layer of particularly iridium-rich clay in sediments 65 million years old, evidence that a vast asteroid impact had put such a cloud of particulates into the atmosphere as to deprive the planet of sunshine, turning it into a wintry vista, and in the process contributing to the demise of the dinosaurs. In the years that followed, it became ever clearer that nuclear weapons, dispatched in the quantities both the United States and USSR had been planning for, would have a similar effect. This prospective phenomenon was dubbed "nuclear winter."

In this way, nuclear extermination would also prove to be an apocalyptic weather event, giving it an affinity with what, in the decades to come, would be called "global warming" and then "climate change." The nuclear story, the first (and at the time the only imaginable) tale of our extinction by our own hands, rose into the news periodically and even into front-page headlines, as during the Cuban Missile Crisis, as well as into the movies and popular culture. Unlike climate change, it was a global catastrophe that could happen at any moment and be carried to its disastrous conclusion in a relatively short period of time, bringing it closer to the today and tomorrow of the news.

Nonetheless, nuclear arsenals, too, were potential life-enders and so news-enders. As a result, most of the time their existence and development managed to translate poorly into daily headlines. For so many of those years in that now long-gone world of the Cold War standoff, the nuclear issue was somehow everywhere, a kind of exterminationist grid over life itself, and yet, like climate change, nowhere at all. Except for a few brief stretches in those decades, antinuclear activists struggled desperately to bring the nuclear issue out of the shadows.

The main arsenals on the planet, still enormous, are now in a kind of nuclear hibernation and are only "news" when, for instance, their very backwater status becomes an issue. This was the case with a spate of headlines about test cheating and drug use scandals involving US Air Force "missileers" who feel that in their present posts they are career los-ers. Most of the major national arsenals are almost never mentioned in the news. They are essentially no-news zones. These would include the gigantic Russian one, the perhaps two hundred weapons in the Israeli arsenal, and those of the British, French, Indians, and Pakistanis (except when it comes to stories about fears of future loose nukes from that country's stock of weapons falling into the hands of terrorists).

The only exceptions in the twenty-first century have been Iran, a country in the spotlight for a decade even though its nuclear program lies somewhere between prospective and imaginary, and North Korea, which continues to develop a modest (but dangerous) arsenal. In contrast, even though a full-scale nuclear war between Pakistan and India—each of which may now have about a hundred nuclear weapons and is adding more—would be a global catastrophe, with nuclear-winter effects that would engulf the planet causing widespread famine, most of the time you simply wouldn't know it. These days, it turns out, we have other problems.

If the end of the world doesn't fit well with "the news," neither does denial. The idea of a futureless humanity is difficult to take in and that has undoubtedly played a role in suppressing the newsiness of both the nuclear situation and climate change. Each is now woven into our lives in essential, if little acknowledged, ways and yet both remain remarkably recessive. Add to that a fatalistic feeling among many that these are issues beyond our capacity to deal with, and you have a potent brew not just for the repression of news but also for the failure to weave what news we do get into a larger picture that we could keep before us as we live our lives. Who, after all, wants to live life like that?

And yet nuclear weapons and climate change are human creations, which means that the problems they represent have human solutions. They are quite literally in our hands. In the case of climate change, we can even point to an example of what can be done about a human-caused global environmental disaster-in-the-making: the "hole" in the ozone layer over Antarctica. Discovered in 1985, it continued to grow for years, threatening a prospective health catastrophe. It was found to be due to the effects of CFC (chlorofluorocarbon) compounds used in air-conditioning units, refrigerators, and aerosol propellants, and then released into the atmosphere. In fact, the nations of the world did come together around CFCs, most of which have now been replaced, and that hole has been reduced, though it isn't expected to heal entirely until much later this century.

Of course, compared with the burning of fossil fuels, the economic and political interests involved in CFCs were minor. Still, the Montreal Protocol on Substances that Deplete the Ozone Layer is evidence that solutions can be reached, however imperfectly, on a global scale when it comes to human-caused environmental problems.

What makes climate change so challenging is that the CO_2 (and methane) being generated by the extraction, production, and burning of fossil fuels supports the most profitable corporations in history, as well as energy states such as Saudi Arabia and Russia that are, in essence, national versions of such corporations. The drive for profits has so far proven unstoppable. Those who run the big oil companies, like the tobacco companies before them, undoubtedly know what potential harm they are doing to us. They know what it will mean for humanity if resources (and profits) aren't poured into alternative energy research and development. And like those cigarette companies, they go right on. They are indeed intent, for instance, on turning North America into "Saudi America," hunting down and extracting major reserves of fossil fuel in the most difficult spots on the planet. Their response to climate change has, in fact, been to put some of their vast profits into the funding of a campaign of climate change denialism and obfuscation and into the coffers of chosen politicians and think tanks willing to lend a hand.

In fact, one of the grim wonders of climate change has been the ability of Big Energy and its lobbyists to politicize an issue that wouldn't normally have a "left" or "right," and to make bad science into an ongoing news story. In other words, an achievement that couldn't be more criminal in nature has also been their great coup de théâtre.

This is the road to hell and it has not been paved with good intentions.

TEN

A Golden Age for Journalism

In 1949, my mother—known in the gossip columns of that era as "New York's girl caricaturist"—was freelancing theatrical sketches to a number of New York's newspapers and magazines, including the *Brooklyn Eagle*. That paper, then more than a century old, had just a few years of life left in it. From 1846 to 1848, its editor had been the poet Walt Whitman. In later years, my mother used to enjoy telling a story about the *Eagle* editor she dealt with who, on learning that I was being sent to Walt Whitman Kindergarten, responded in the classically gruff newspaper manner memorialized in movies like *His Girl Friday*: "Are they still naming things after that old bastard?"

In my childhood, New York City was, you might say, papered with newspapers. The *Daily News, Daily Mirror, Herald Tribune, Wall Street Journal.* There were perhaps nine or ten significant papers on newsstands every day and, though that might bring to mind some golden age of journalism, it's worth remembering that a number of them were already amalgams. The *Journal-American*, for instance, had once been the *Evening Journal* and the *American*, just as the *World-Telegram & Sun* had been a threesome, the *World*, the *Evening Telegram*, and the *Sun*. In my own household, we read the *New York Times* (disappointingly comic-strip-less), the *New York Post* (then a liberal, not right-wing, rag that ran

"Pogo" and Herblock's political cartoons), and sometimes the *Journal-American* (home of "Ripley's Believe It or Not!" and "The Phantom").

Then there were always the magazines: in our house, *Life*, the *Saturday Evening Post*, *Look*, the *New Yorker*—my mother worked for some of them, too—and who knows what else in a roiling mass of print. It was a paper universe all the way to the horizon, though change and competition were in the air. After all, the screen (the TV screen, that is) was entering the American home like gangbusters. Mine arrived in 1953 when the *Post* assigned my mother to draw the Army-McCarthy hearings, which—something new under the sun—were to be televised live by ABC.

Still, at least in my hometown, it seemed distinctly like a golden age of print news, if not of journalism. Some might reserve that label for the shakeup, breakdown era of the 1960s, that moment when the so-called New Journalism arose, an alternative press burst onto the scene, and, for a brief moment in the late 1960s and early 1970s, the old journalism put its mind to uncovering massacres, revealing the worst of American war, reporting on Washington-style scandal, and taking down a president. In the meantime, magazines like *Esquire* and *Harper's* came to specialize in the sort of chip-on-the-shoulder, stylish voiciness that would, one day, become the hallmark of the online world and the age of the Internet. (I still remember the thrill of reading Tom Wolfe's *The Kandy-Kolored Tangerine-Flake Streamline Baby* on the world of custom cars, a book that first appeared as a series of essays in *Harper's*. It put the vrrrooom into writing in a dazzling way.)

However, it took the arrival of the twenty-first century to turn the journalistic world of the 1950s upside down and point it toward the trash heap of history. I'm talking about the years that shrank the screen and put it first on your desk, then in your hand, next in your pocket, and already, for some, even in your eyeglasses—and made it the way you connected with everyone on Earth and they—whether as friends, enemies, the curious, voyeurs, corporate sellers and buyers, or the NSA—with you. Only then did it became apparent that, throughout the print era, all those years of paper running off presses and newsboys and newsstands, from Walt Whitman to Bob Woodward and Carl Bernstein, the newspaper had been misnamed.

Journalism's amour propre had overridden a clear-eyed assessment of what exactly the paper really was. Only then would it be fully apparent that it always should have been called the "adpaper." When the corporation and the "mad men" who worked for it spied the Internet and saw how conveniently it gathered audiences and what you could learn about their lives, preferences, and most intimate buying habits, the ways you could slice and dice demographics and sidle up to potential customers just behind the ever-present screen, the ad began to flee print for the online world. It was then, of course, that newspapers (as well as magazines)—left with overworked, ever-smaller staffs, evaporating funding, and the ad-less news—began to shudder, shrink, and in some cases collapse (as they might not have done if the news had been what fled).

New York still has four dailies (the *Post*, the *Daily News*, the *New York Times*, and the *Wall Street Journal*). However, in recent years, many two-paper towns such as Denver and Seattle morphed into far shakier one-paper towns as papers like the *Rocky Mountain News* and the *Seattle Post-Intelligencer* passed out of existence (or into digital-only existence). Meanwhile, the *Detroit News* and *Detroit Free Press* went over to a three-day-a-week home delivery print edition, and the *Times-Picayune* of New Orleans went down to a three-day-a-week schedule (before returning as a four-day *Picayune* and a three-day-a-week tabloid in 2013). The *Christian Science Monitor* stopped publishing a weekday paper altogether. And so it went. In those years, newspaper advertising took a terrible hit, circulation declined, sometimes precipitously, and bankruptcies were the order of the day.

The least self-supporting sections, especially book reviews, simply evaporated and in the one place of significance that a book review remained, the *New York Times*, the section shrank. Sunday magazines shriveled up. Billionaires began to buy papers at bargain-basement prices as, in essence, vanity projects. Jobs and staffs were radically cut (as were the TV versions of the same so that, for example, if you tune in to NBC's *Nightly News* with Brian Williams, you often have the feeling that the estimable Richard Engel, with the job title of chief foreign correspondent, is the only "foreign correspondent" still on the job, flown eternally from hot spot to hot spot around the globe).

No question about it, if you were an established reporter of a certain age or anyone who worked in a newsroom, this was the aluminum age of journalism. Your job might be in jeopardy—along with your pension, too. In these years, stunned by what was suddenly happening to them, the management of papers stood for a time frozen in place like proverbial deer in the headlights as the voiciness of the Internet broke over them, turning their op-ed pages into the grey sisters of the reading world. Then, in a blinding rush to save what could be saved, recapture the missing ad, or find any other path to a new model of profitability from digital advertising (disappointing) to paywalls (a mixed bag), papers rushed online. In the process, they doubled the work of the remaining journalists and editors, who were now to service both the new newspaper and the old.

In so many ways, it's been, and continues to be, a sad, even horrific, tale of loss. A similar tale of woe involves the printed book. Its only advantage: there were no ads to flee the premises, but it suffered nonetheless—already largely crowded out of the newspaper as a non–revenue producer and out of consciousness by a blitz of new ways of reading and being entertained. And I say that as someone who has spent most of his life as an editor of print books. The keening and mourning about the fall of print journalism has gone on for years. It's a development that represents—depending on who's telling the story—the end of an age, the fall of all standards, or the loss of civic spirit and the sort of investigative coverage that might keep a few more politicians and corporate heads honest.

Let's admit that the sins of the Internet are legion and well-known: the massive programs of government surveillance it enables, the corporate surveillance it ensures, the loss of privacy it encourages, the flamers and trolls it births, the conspiracy theorists, angry men, and strange characters to whom it gives a seemingly endless moment in the sun, and the way, among other things, it tends to sort like and like together in a self-reinforcing loop of opinion. Yes, yes, it's all true, all unnerving.

As the editor of the website TomDispatch.com, I've spent the last decade-plus plunged into just that world, often with people half my age or younger. I don't tweet. I don't have a Kindle or the equivalent. I don't even have a smart phone or a tablet of any sort. When something—anything—goes wrong with my computer, I feel like a doomed figure in an alien universe, wish for the last machine I understood (a typewriter), and then throw myself on the mercy of my daughter.

I've been overwhelmed, especially at the height of the Bush years, by cookie-cutter hate email—sometimes scores or hundreds of them at a time—of a sort that would make your skin crawl. I've been threatened. I've repeatedly received abusive emails, blasts of red-hot anger that would startle anyone, because the Internet, so my experience tells me, loosens inhibitions, wipes out taboos, and encourages a sense of anonymity that in the older world of print, letters, or face-to-face meetings would have been far less likely to take center stage. I've seen plenty that's disturbed me. So you'd think, given my age, my background, and my present life, that I, too, might be in mourning for everything that's going, going, gone, everything we've lost.

But I have to admit it: I have another feeling that, at a purely personal level, outweighs all of the above. In terms of journalism, of expression, of voice, of fine reporting and superb writing, of a range of news, thoughts, views, perspectives, and opinions about places, worlds, and phenomena that I wouldn't otherwise have known about, there has never been a moment like this. I'm in awe. Despite everything, despite every malign purpose to which the Internet is being put, I consider it a wonder of our age. Yes, perhaps it is the age from hell for traditional reporters and editors working double-time, online and off, for newspapers that are crumbling, but for enterprising readers, can there be any doubt that now, not the 1840s or the 1930s or the 1960s, is the golden age of journalism?

The press today is, in a way, the upbeat twin of NSA surveillance. Just as the NSA can reach anyone, so, in a different sense, can you. Which also means, if you're a website, anyone can, at least theoretically, find and read you. (In my experience, I'm often amazed at who can and does.) And you, the reader, have in remarkable profusion the finest writing on the planet at your fingertips. You can read around the world almost without limit, follow your favorite writers to the ends of the earth.

The problem of this moment isn't too little. It's not a collapsing world. It's way too much. These days, in a way that was never previously imaginable, it's possible to drown in provocative and illuminating writing and reporting, framing and opining. In fact, it's a constant challenge, whatever the subject and whatever your expertise, simply to keep up.

The Rise of the Reader

In the 1960s and early 1970s, in the "golden age of journalism," I read the *New York Times* (as I still do in print daily), various magazines ranging from the *New Yorker* and *Ramparts* to "underground" papers like the *Great Speckled Bird* when they happened to fall into my hands, and *I. F. Stone's Weekly* (to which I subscribed), as well as James Ridgeway and Andrew Kopkind's *Hard Times*, among other publications of the moment. Somewhere in those years or thereafter, I also subscribed to a once-a-week paper that had the best of the *Guardian*, the *Washington Post*, and *Le Monde* in it. For the time, that covered a fair amount of ground.

Still, the limits of that "golden" moment couldn't be more obvious now. Today, after all, if I care to, I can read online every word of the *Guardian*, *Washington Post*, and *Le Monde*. And that's every single day— and that, in turn, is nothing.

It's all out there for you. Most of the major dailies and magazines of the globe, trade publications, propaganda outfits, Pentagon handouts, the voiciest of blogs, specialist websites, the websites of individual experts with a great deal to say, websites, in fact, for just about anyone from historians, theologians, and philosophers to techies, book lovers, and yes, those fascinated with journalism. You can read your way through the American press and the world press. You can read whole papers as their editors put them together or—at least in your mind—you can become the editor of your own op-ed page every day of the week, three times, six times a day if you like (and odds are that it will be more interesting to you, and perhaps others, than the op-ed offerings of any specific paper you might care to mention). You can essentially curate your own newspaper or magazine. Or—a particular blessing in the present ocean of words—you can rely on a new set of people out there who have superb collection and curating abilities, as well as fascinating editorial eyes. I'm talking about teams of people at what I like to call "riot sites"—for the wild profusion of headlines they sport—like Antiwar.com (where no story worth reading about conflict on our planet seems to go unnoticed) or Real Clear Politics. You can subscribe to an almost endless range of curated online newsletters targeted to specific subjects, like the "morning brief" that comes to me every weekday filled with recommended pieces on cyberwar, terrorism, surveillance, and the like from the Center on National Security at Fordham Law School. And I'm not even mentioning the online versions of your favorite print magazine, or purely online magazines such as Salon.com, or the many websites I visit, including Truthout, AlterNet, Common Dreams, and TruthDig, which feature their own pieces and picks. And in mentioning all of this, I'm barely scratching the surface of the world of writing that interests me.

There has, in fact, never been a do-it-yourself moment like this when it comes to journalism and coverage of the world. Period. For the first time in history, you and I have been put in the position of the newspaper editor. We're no longer simply passive readers at the mercy of someone else's idea of how to "cover" or organize this planet and its many moving parts. To one degree or another, to the extent that any of us have the time, curiosity, or energy, all of us can have a hand in shaping, reimagining, and understanding our world in new ways.

Yes, it is a journalistic universe from hell, a genuine nightmare. And yet, for a reader, it's also an experimental world, something thrillingly, unexpectedly new under the sun. For that reader, a strangely democratic and egalitarian Era of the Word has emerged. It's chaotic, it's too much, and it's also an unstable brew likely to morph into god knows what. Still, perhaps someday, amid its inanities and horrors, it will also be remembered, at least for a brief historical moment, as a golden age of the reader—a time when all the words you could ever have needed were freely offered up for you to curate as you wish.

AFTERWORD

Letter to an Unknown Whistleblower

Dear Whistleblower,

I don't know who you are or what you do or how old you may be. I just know that you exist somewhere in our future as surely as does tomorrow or next year. You may be young and computer-savvy or a career federal employee well along in years. You might be someone who entered government service filled with idealism or who signed on to "the bureaucracy" just to make a living. You may be a libertarian, a closet left-winger, or as mainstream and down-the-center as it's possible to be.

I don't know much, but I know one thing that you may not yet know yourself. I know that you're there. I know that, just as Edward Snowden and Chelsea Manning did, you will, for reasons of your own, feel compelled to take radical action, to put yourself in danger. When the time comes, you will know that this is what you must do, that this is why you find yourself where you are, and then you're going to tell us plenty that has been kept from us about how our government really operates. You are going to shock us to the core.

And how exactly do I know this? Because despite our striking inability to predict the future, it's a no-brainer that the national security state is already building you into its labyrinthine systems. In the urge of its officials to control all of us and every situation, in their mania for all-encompassing secrecy, in their classification not just of the millions of documents they generate, but essentially all of their operations as "secret" or "top secret," in their all-encompassing urge to shut off the most essential workings of the government from the eyes of its citizenry, in their escalating urge to punish anyone who would bring their secret activities to light, in their urge to see or read or listen in on or peer into the lives of you (every "you" on the planet), in their urge to build a global surveillance state and a military that will dominate everything in or out of its path, in their urge to drop bombs on Pakistan and fire missiles at Syria, in their urge to be able to assassinate just about anyone just about anywhere robotically, they are birthing you.

For every action, a reaction. So they say, no?

Give our national security managers credit, though: they may prove to be the master builders of the early twenty-first century. Their ambitions have been breathtaking and their ability to commandeer staggering amounts of our taxpayer dollars to pay for those projects hardly less so. Their monuments to themselves, their version of pyramids and ziggurats—like the vast data storage center the NSA is building in Bluffdale, Utah, to keep a yottabyte of private information about all of us, or the new post-9/11 headquarters of the National Geospatial-Intelligence Agency—are in their own way unique. In their urge to control everything, to see everything from your Facebook chatter to the emails of the Brazilian president, they are creating a system built to blowback, and not just from the outside or distant lands.

Chalmers Johnson, who took "blowback," an obscure term of CIA tradecraft, and embedded it in our everyday language, would have instantly recognized what they're doing: creating a blowback machine whose "unintended consequences" (another term of his) are guaranteed, like the effects of the Snowden revelations, to stun us all in a myriad of ways.

They have built their system so elaborately, so expansively, and their ambitions have been so grandiose that they have had no choice but to embed you in their developing global security state, deep in the entrails of their secret world—tens of thousands of possible yous, in fact. Yous galore, all of whom see some part, some corner, of the world that is curtained off from the rest of us. And because they have built using the power of tomorrow, they have created a situation in which the prospective whistleblower, the leaker of tomorrow, has access not just to a few pieces of paper but to files beyond imagination. They, not you, have prepared the way for future mass document dumps, for staggering releases, of a sort that once upon time in a far more modest system based largely on paper would have been inconceivable.

They have, that is, paved the way for everything that you are one day guaranteed to do. Worse yet (for them), they have created a world populated with tens of thousands of people, often young, often nomadic in job terms, and often with remarkable computer skills who have access to parts of their vast system, to unknown numbers of secret programs and documents, and the many things from phone calls to emails to credit card transactions to social media interactions to biometric data that they so helpfully store away.

And it doesn't matter what they, in their post-Snowden panic, may do to try to prevent you from accessing their system. None of the new rules and programs they are installing to prevent the next Edward Snowden or Chelsea Manning from collecting anything right down to the national security equivalent of the kitchen sink will stop you. After all, you may even be one of the ones they have chosen to install those safeguards, to put those measures in place. You may be one of the ones they have specially trained in the intricacies and failsafe mechanisms of their system.

And here's the uncanny thing about you: just doing what comes naturally, you will overcome any measures they try to install and make a mockery of any measures or training programs they put in place to help your coworkers spot you. Almost by definition, they won't be able to find you until it's too late. You'll display none of the traits that someone about to betray their world should exhibit. And no wonder, since you'll be one of the many recognizable cogs in their machinery until almost the moment—already too late in the game for them—when you aren't.

You are, in that sense, the perfect double agent. Until you, in essence, become a spy for the American people, for the old democratic system in which government was the people's property and those we elect were supposed to let us know what they were doing in our name, you aren't just masquerading as one of them, you are one of them.

I have no way of knowing what will first strike you as wrong. I just know that something will. It might be very specific and close at hand—

something amiss you see in the program you're working on, some outrageous expenditure of money or set of lies about what an agency or outfit is doing, or some act or set of acts that you, while growing up, had
been taught were un-American. The possibilities are legion. After all, the
national security state that they've built and engorged with taxpayer dollars, using fear and the excuse of American "safety," has dispatched armies
and special operations forces and drones all over the world to commit
mayhem and increase global instability, to kill civilians, wipe out wedding
parties, kidnap and torture the innocent, assassinate by robot, and so on.

Or maybe it all just sneaks up on you, the wrongness of it. Maybe,
even if you're too young to remember the totalitarian states of the previous century, something about the urge of our national security managers to create total systems of control, trump the law, and do as they
please in the name of their need for knowledge will simply get under
your skin. You'll know that this isn't the way it was supposed to be.

At some point, it will just creep you out, and even though until that
moment you didn't know it, you'll be ready. They won't be able to avoid
you. They won't be able to eliminate you. They won't even be able to find
you. You are, after all, part of their landscape, like the grass on the hillside
or the steps to a house.

Manning and Snowden were the first harbingers of the new world
of whistleblowing. Snowden learned from Manning and other whistleblowers who preceded him and were persecuted by the state. You will
learn from all of them. Each was a small tornado-like version of the blowback machine they are still in the process of creating. Each changed how
the world looks at America and how many of us look at ourselves. Each
put in place some small part of the foundation for a world in which such
a blowback machine would not be the creation of choice for those with
the money and power to build monuments to themselves. Each was a
raging embarrassment, a dent in the amour propre of the national security state. Each was an insult to its ability to control much of anything,
including itself.

Those running the government and many who write about you in
the mainstream will revile you. You will be denounced as a traitor, a defector, a criminal, and your acts called treasonous, even if you're one of
the last hopes of the American republic. Right now, those like you are

sure to be prosecuted, jailed, or chased implacably across the planet. But this won't last forever. Someday, your country will recognize what you did—first of all for yourself, for your own sense of what's decent and right in this world, and then for us—as the acts of an upright and even heroic American.

In the meantime, just remember: the national security state is a giant blowback machine and you, whoever you are, will be part of the remedy to it.

ACKNOWLEDGMENTS

This book would not exist without my editor and friend Anthony Arnove. It's no more complicated than that. He made my scattered texts of these last years into an actual book and should, in some sense, be considered its author as much as I am. There's no way to thank him enough. Let me not forget the rest of the folks at Haymarket books either: Dao X. Tran, Sarah Grey, Rachel Cohen, Eric Kerl, Jim Plank, Rory Fanning, John McDonald, Julie Fain, and that superb copyeditor Caroline Luft. They make books that look like jewels.

Next comes the crew at TomDispatch.com. The world would be a lesser place in a million and one ways without them: Nick Turse, my companion-in-arms in these last years (and I, his social secretary for the mail that constantly comes into the site addressed to him); Andy Kroll, one of the crackerjack young reporters of our moment, who somehow finds the time to lend a hand and save me eternally from myself; Erika Eichelberger, another journalistic up-and-comer, who keeps our social media in a state of grace; Christopher Holmes, who adds generosity to an eagle eye; and Joe Duax and Novaid Khan, always on the spot when needed.

In addition, a giant bow of thanks is in order for Patrick Lannan and the folks at Lannan Foundation, who have, over the years, made TomDispatch their concern in a way that truly matters. Then there's Taya Kitman, my empathetic partner at the Nation Institute, who has been ever supportive, and Annelise Whitley, who is ever efficient.

A special bow to two friends, Jonathan Cobb and Jim Peck, who regularly make my thinking, and so my writing, sharper—and a sad acknowledgment that the third person I would have included in this list, Jonathan Schell, is no longer here to thank.

Appreciation should go as well to all my reposting pals at other websites—too many to name—who make sure that TomDispatch pieces, mine included, are spread across the universe of the Internet.

Next in line, my wife, Nancy, my children, Will and Maggie, my son-in-law, Chris, and my grandson, Charlie: the older I get the more all of you mean to me.

Finally, Edward Snowden and Glenn Greenwald—and, in fact, all the whistleblowers and leakers (and the journalists they've entrusted with their information) who have put themselves on the line in these last years to ensure that this American world of ours doesn't disappear into a locked room to which we have no admittance. They deserve our thanks, big time.

A NOTE ON THE TEXT

The pieces that make up this book were written between the end of 2011 and April 2014 for my website, TomDispatch.com. These were the years when the power of the national security state in Washington came into particularly striking focus. They were the years in which Americans became aware that the National Security Agency was building a global surveillance regime and, in the process, was treating this country as if it were just another foreign land. Americans were, that is, being surveilled on a previously unimaginable scale. Above all, of course, from June 2013 on, we were in the year of living Snowdenly—and what an experience that's been.

It's important to note that the essays included here are not simply the originals I wrote. They were edited, trimmed, or cut down, modestly updated, and woven into book form. The telltale signs of the immediate moment—all the uses of "recently" and "next week," along with examples that were gripping then but are forgotten today—have been removed, as have most of the thematic repetitions that are bound to pop up in any set of weekly responses to ongoing events. Nothing basic or significant about them has, however, been changed; for better or worse, nothing had to be, which tells you something about our present world.

Though this text generally (though not always) moves chronologically within its chapters, I haven't included the original date on which each piece was posted. I'd rather it flowed, as I think it does, as a book-reading experience. You can find and check out the originals, however, at the TomDispatch website (http://www.tomdispatch.com) simply by putting a few words of any passage into the search window there. When you go to those originals, you'll also undoubtedly note that, while the book has no footnotes, the originals are heavily sourced in the way that the Internet makes possible—via links in the text. These will lead you to both my sources and also sometimes suggestions for further exploration. Linking is, in fact, the first democratic form of footnoting, making sources instantly accessible to normal readers who, unlike scholars, may not have ready access to a good library. URLs in a book, however, are both cumbersome and useless. So if you want to check my sources, you'll need to go to the originals online at TomDispatch.com. Fair warning, however: One of the debits of linking is that links regularly die, so the older the piece, the greater the chance that some of the links won't work.

INDEX

"Passim" (literally "scattered") indicates intermittent discussion of a topic over a cluster of pages.

Abrams, Creighton, 78
Abu Ghraib prison, 61, 88, 90
Act of Valor, 26
advertising, 151, 152
Afghanistan, 9, 23, 25, 36–39 passim, 47, 93, 101–4 passim, 114; army, 71; drones in, 97, 98; First Afghan War, 51–52; invasion of 2001, 53, 113; private contractors in, 81; US "drawing down," 69; US expenditures, 69, 71; US "Salt Pit" prison, 88; wedding party massacres, 74, 75
Africa, 9, 26, 54, 97, 98, 132. *See also* Egypt; Libya; Mali; Somalia
agents provocateurs, 83
aircraft carriers, 98, 99, 100, 105, 116
All-Volunteer Force (AVF), 78–81 passim
al-Qaeda, 23, 36, 51–55 passim, 72, 101, 116, 133; drone campaigns against, 9, 51, 54, 74; North Africa, 9, 119; as Satan, 5; September 11 attacks, 112
al-Shabab, 102, 133
alternative energy, 140–41

alternative press, 77, 150, 154
American citizens, US assassination of. *See* US citizens, US assassination of
American exceptionalism, 67, 122–23
American public opinion. *See* public opinion, American
anticommunism, 41
Antiwar.com, 154
antiwar movement: Vietnam War, 77–78, 83, 84
Arkin, William, 14, 22, 81
arms trade, 8, 92
assassination, 24, 26, 66, 88–89, 127, 132, 135, 158. *See also* drone assassinations
automobile accident deaths. *See* vehicular deaths
Awlaki, Anwar al-, 51, 130

Bacevich, Andrew, 78, 79
Bamford, James, 21, 109
Becker, Jo, 131–32
Bin Laden, Osama, 24, 26, 33–40 passim, 52, 96, 116, 119, 130
"black sites" (prisons). *See* secret prisons
"blowback" (word), 50, 158
"blowback machine," 105, 158, 160, 161
Bluffdale, Utah, 15, 21, 45, 158
Bolton, John, 112

book industry. *See* publishing industry

Boundless Informant, 10

Brazil, 45, 48, 93, 94, 117

Brennan, John O., 35, 50, 51, 55, 122, 123, 133, 134

Britain. *See* United Kingdom

Brooklyn Eagle, 149

Brzezinski, Zbigniew, 52

Bush, George H. W., 111, 112

Bush, George W.: administration, 23, 35, 53, 86, 87; CIA relations, 38, 53; drone policy, 70, 131; Iraq, 54, 101, 128; "personal scorecard," 132–33; September 11 attacks, 41, 53, 127–28

car accidents, fatal. *See* vehicular deaths

carbon dioxide emissions, 38, 140–44 passim, 148

Carter, Jimmy, 140–41

cartoons and comics, 42, 149–50

Casey, William, 51

Caslen, Robert L., 120

Castro, Fidel, 26, 132

casualties, civilian. *See* civilian casualties

cell phones, 8, 21, 44

Center on National Security, 154–55

Central Intelligence Agency (CIA), 17, 18, 22–25 passim, 51–56 passim, 83–89 passim, 96–101 passim, 134; assassination, 132; drones, 35, 54, 83–84, 89, 96–101 passim, 105, 119, 122, 134; Libya operations, 118–19; president's private army, 51, 97, 117, 130; "Worldwide Attack Matrix" plan, 38

CFCs. *See* chlorofluorocarbons (CFCs)

chemical weapons, 39, 41, 68

Cheney, Dick, 7, 24, 40, 41, 64, 112, 127–28

children: killed in drone attacks, 70, 89, 125; Obama claims concern for, 67, 68

China, 23, 33, 40–41, 92–96 passim, 111, 117; ancient, 61; drones, 124; military, 100, 116; US intelligence target, 130; Vietnam War, 118

chlorofluorocarbons (CFCs), 147, 148

CIA. *See* Central Intelligence Agency (CIA)

cigarette industry. *See* tobacco industry

civilian casualties, 70, 72–76 passim, 89, 125, 133

Clapper, James, 14, 65, 89–90

classified documents, 8, 62, 63, 64, 106, 158. *See also* Manning, Chelsea; Snowden, Edward

climate change. *See* global warming

Cold War, 12, 18, 30, 40–41, 79, 93, 111; end of, 91, 118; "moles," 46; nuclear weapons, 145–46

comics and cartoons. *See* cartoons and comics

conscripted military forces. *See* draft military forces

Congo, 26, 132

Congress, US. *See* US Congress

"conspiracy" (word), 46

corporate cover-up, 139

corporate-military complex, 80–81, 90. *See also* military-industrial complex

counterinsurgency, 54, 95, 104

"covert" (word), 26–27, 89, 122, 131–32

cover-up, corporate. *See* corporate cover-up

criminal evidence, destruction of. *See* destruction of evidence

Cuba, 17, 26, 132, 146

cyberstalking of "love interests," 90

cyberwar, 7, 15, 61, 114, 116, 135

data-mining, 10, 21, 44, 48, 58; official denial of, 89

data-storage centers, 15, 21, 45, 158

Defense Clandestine Services (DCS), 23–24, 130

Defense Department. *See* US Department of Defense

Defense Intelligence Agency (DIA), 18, 21, 24, 25, 63, 83

"defense" spending. *See* military spending

delusion and denial, 89, 107, 114, 115,

138, 139, 148
Dempsey, Martin, 117
Department of Homeland Security
    (DHS). *See* US Department of
    Homeland Security (DHS)
Department of Justice. *See* US Department
    of Justice
Department of State. *See* US Department
    of State
desertion and mutiny, 71, 77
destruction of evidence, 87–88
detention, extralegal. *See* "rendition";
    secret prisons
DeYoung, Karen, 50
DIA. *See* Defense Intelligence Agency
    (DIA)
Director of National Intelligence. *See*
    Office of the Director of National
    Intelligence
Dirty Wars (Scahill), 41–42
"disaster capitalism," 95
"dissidents," 2, 30–31, 33
Djibouti, 98
DNA, 12
do-it-yourself journalism, 154–55
Dozier, Kimberly, 62
doublespeak, 90, 123
draft military forces, 77–79 passim
drone assassinations, 35, 51, 76, 83–85
    passim, 89, 99, 122, 130–34 passim;
    bin Laden, 96, 119; "bloodlessness,"
    63; "legality," 123, 127, 130, 134
drones and drone wars, 7, 9, 23–26 pas-
    sim, 35–39 passim, 76–77, 81–82,
    96–99 passim, 105, 120–25 passim;
    Libya, 102; Niger, 54; Pakistan, 26,
    70, 97, 101; Saudi Arabia, 51; target
    wedding parties, 72–76 passim

Egypt, 10–11, 86
Ehrenfreund, Max, 21–22
email, 31, 153
"enemy-industrial complex," 36–42
energy production and use, 94, 95, 137–42
    passim, 148

Engel, Richard, 151
environment, 94–95, 137–48
Espionage Act, 31, 57, 64
Europe, 44, 48, 93, 100, 114, 143. *See also*
    France; Germany; Italy; Russia;
    United Kingdom
evidence destruction. *See* destruction of
    evidence
exceptionalism, American. *See* American
    exceptionalism
executive power, 26, 39, 88–89, 97–98,
    105, 117, 127–36 passim
extralegal rendition of suspects. *See* ren-
    dition, extralegal

Federal Bureau of Investigation (FBI),
    13, 83, 84
federal employees as whistleblowers. *See*
    whistleblowers
Fifth Amendment, 65, 133–34
films, 26
financial crisis, 93, 128
First Amendment, 10, 65
foreign correspondents, 151
Foreign Intelligence Surveillance Act
    (FISA) court, 14, 33–34, 84–85
fossil fuels, 94, 95, 138–44 passim, 148.
    See also oil
Fourth Amendment, 10, 65
fracking, 95, 139
"fraggings," 77
France, 77, 79, 122, 147
Freidersdorf, Conor, 6

gag orders, 13
geospatial intelligence (GEOINT), 19–20
Geospatial-Intelligence Agency. *See* Na-
    tional Geospatial-Intelligence Agency
Germany, 45, 110
"global security state," 10–15 passim, 29,
    61, 66, 158
global warming, 138, 139, 142–46 passim
Global War on Terror (GWOT), 7, 36,
    69, 85, 86, 114, 128; declaration of,
    53, 112; replaced by "Global War

on You," 66
Gorbachev, Mikhail, 52
government documents, classified. *See*
classified documents
government employees as whistleblowers.
See whistleblowers
government lying. *See* lies and lying
government spending. *See* intelligence
spending; military spending
Great Britain. *See* United Kingdom
Greenwald, Glenn, 1–2, 29, 64, 133–34
Gulf War, 112, 113
guns, 37–38

Hale, Nathan, 55–56, 59
Hansen, James, 138
Hard Measures (Rodriguez), 87–88
Heinl, Robert D., Jr., 77
Hersh, Seymour, 24
Heyns, Christof, 89
Homeland Security Department. *See* US
Department of Homeland Security
(DHS)
Hussein, Saddam, 41, 52, 102, 112
hypersonic weapons, 99

Ignatius, David, 124
India, 11, 44–45, 94, 117, 147
industrial-military complex. *See* military-
industrial complex
information overload, 153, 155
informing and informants, 31, 63–64, 83
Insider Threat Program, 63–64
intelligence, geospatial. *See* geospatial
intelligence (GEOINT)
intelligence building complexes, 8, 20,
22, 56
intelligence spending, 14–15, 20, 22, 45,
83, 117
Intergovernmental Panel on Climate
Change, 143
Internet, 21, 44, 48, 151–55 passim, 158,
159
interventionism, 112, 118–20; Obama,
67, 68, 102; Reagan, 80. *See also*

Afghanistan; Iraq
The Invisible Government (Wise and
Rose), 17–21 passim, 26
Iran, 7, 10, 17, 23, 36, 69, 113, 116, 128;
drones, 97, 124; Iraq relations, 120;
nuclear weapons, 147; US intelligence target, 130
Iraq, 8, 9, 38–42 passim, 47, 52–54
passim, 68–71 passim, 93, 101–4
passim, 112–14 passim, 119–20;
assassination in, 24; drones in, 97,
98; private contractors in, 81;
special operations in, 24, 25, 98;
US-built embassies in, 24, 71;
victory declared in, 54; wedding
party massacres, 74. *See also* Abu
Ghraib prison; Gulf War
Islam. *See* Muslims
Israel, 147
Italy, 86

Japan, 93, 96, 100, 110, 145
Johnson, Chalmers, 51, 158
Joint Special Operations Command
(JSOC), 24, 25, 39, 117
Jordan, 10
journalism. *See* news media
journalism, DIY. *See* do-it-yourself jour-
nalism
Justice Department. *See* US Department
of Justice

Karzai, Hamid, 103, 104
Kerry, John, 103–4
Keystone XL pipeline, 143
Khalilzad, Zalmay, 112
kidnapping, 32, 70, 85, 86, 100, 102
"kill lists," 7, 35, 125, 131–34 passim
Kilpatrick, David, 119
Kim, Stephen, 90
Kiriakou, John, 87, 90
Klare, Michael, 139
Koh, Harold H., 134
Korean War, 129
Kuwait, 52

Lady, Robert Seldon, 86
law, 104, 160; drone use justification, 35–
    36, 121, 123, 127, 130, 134; secret,
    50, 85. *See also* Espionage Act;
    "rendition"
leaks, news. *See* news leaks
Levin, Carl, 84
Libya, 9, 39, 102, 118–19
Lichtblau, Eric, 33–34
lies and lying, 6, 58, 89–90, 160
Los Angeles Times, 83–84
"love interests," cyberstalking of. *See*
    cyberstalking of "love interests"
Lumumba, Patrice, 26, 132
Luxemburg, Rosa, 2

magazines, 150, 154
Mali, 39, 54, 102, 119
Manning, Chelsea, 56, 57, 63, 90, 107, 157
Matthews, Jennifer, 25
McChrystal, Stanley, 25
McCone, John, 18
media, 26. *See also* Internet; magazines;
    news media
Menendez, Bob, 67
militarization, 23, 25, 118, 120, 130
military bases, 11, 92, 93, 96–97, 99–100,
    115; Iraq, 70, 102, 113; Okinawa,
    96; Qatar, 54; Saudi Arabia, 50–55
    passim
military-corporate complex. *See* corporate-
    military complex
military forces, draft. *See* draft military
    forces
military forces, special operations. *See*
    special operations forces
military forces, volunteer. *See* volunteer
    military forces
military-industrial complex, 7, 80, 120
military reserves, 78
military spending, 69, 71, 82, 92, 100, 116
Miller, Greg, 24, 50, 119, 123
Montreal Protocol on Substances that
    Deplete the Ozone Layer, 148

Morales, Evo, 32, 33
Muhammed, Khalid Sheikh, 87
Muslims, 2, 23, 52, 68, 101, 113; Mali,
    119; United States, 83
Mussa, Amr, 101
"mutually assured destruction" (MAD),
    145–46
mutiny and desertion. *See* desertion and
    mutiny

National Counterterrorism Center
    (NCTC), 21
National Geospatial-Intelligence Agency,
    19–20, 56, 83, 158
National Insider Threat Program. *See*
    Insider Threat Program
National Reconnaissance Office (NRO),
    21–22
national security: "balance" with privacy
    and freedom, 4, 66, 106; as pretext,
    24, 128; as religion, 4–7, 42, 134;
    spending on, 36, 39, 66
National Security Agency (NSA), 1–2, 10,
    15–22 passim, 43–49 passim, 65–66,
    82–85 passim, 89–90, 114; classified
    documents, 107; Internet as "upbeat
    twin" of, 153; Snowden in, 1, 29–30;
    Utah repository, 15, 21, 45, 158
National Security Council, 40, 130
National Security Letters, 13, 14, 83
NATO. *See* North Atlantic Treaty Organ-
    ization (NATO)
NCTC. *See* National Counterterrorism
    Center (NCTC)
"New Journalism," 150
news leaks, 26, 29, 31, 43, 62, 63, 87,
    106–7, 159
news media, 31–32, 40, 62–63, 73–74,
    149–55; on alternative energy, 140–
    41; on climate change, 142–45; on
    drone assassinations, 89; "embed-
    ding" of, 80; GI press, 77; on nuclear
    weapons, 146–47. *See also* news
    leaks; newspapers; news sources
newspapers, 72–73, 77, 149–54 passim.

See also *New York Times*; *Washington Post*
newspeak, 90
news sources, 32, 34, 55, 63
Newtown, Connecticut, school shooting, 2012. *See* Sandy Hook Elementary School shooting, 2012
New York Post, 72–73, 149–50
New York Times, 33–34, 40, 55, 131–32, 149
1984 (Orwell), 109–10
Nixon, Richard, 78, 85
North Atlantic Treaty Organization (NATO), 71, 93, 119
North Korea, 23, 116, 118, 147
NRO. *See* National Reconnaissance Office (NRO)
NSA. *See* National Security Agency (NSA)
nuclear weapons, 100, 145–48
"nuclear winter," 146, 147

Obama, Barack, 35, 43–50 passim, 127–36 passim; Afghanistan, 9, 114; "assassin in chief," 51, 89, 125, 133, 135; China, 94; drone policy, 70, 74, 97, 102, 119–22 passim, 130–33 passim; inaction on torture, 86–87; intelligence policy, 21; interventionism, 67, 68, 102; Iraq, 120; retirement of "war on terror," 66; "sunshine administration," 83–84; suppression of news, 50; on trusting Congress, 64; on trusting NSA, 13; whistleblower prosecutions, 30, 31, 46
Office of the Director of National Intelligence, 21
oil, 52, 113, 128, 138–42 passim
Okinawa, 96
Orwell, George, 46, 85, 90, 109–10
ozone layer hole, 147–48

Pakistan, 10, 69, 97, 135; drone attacks on, 26, 35, 70, 89, 97, 101, 123, 125; nuclear weapons, 147

Panetta, Leon, 50, 89
paramilitarization, 23, 100
"patriot" (word), 64
"peak oil," 138
"Pearl Harbor II," 37, 40
Peck, James, 40–41
Pentagon. *See* US Department of Defense
perjury, 89–90
Persian Gulf, 98, 112, 141. *See also* Gulf War
Petraeus, David, 9, 50, 98
petroleum. *See* oil
phone records and monitoring, 9, 21, 31, 32, 34, 44, 48, 49
phone tapping. *See* wiretapping
planetary degradation, 94–95. *See also* "terracide"
Poitras, Laura, 29
pollution, 95
presidential power. *See* executive power
press. *See* alternative press; magazines; newspapers
Priest, Dana, 14, 22, 81
PRISM (surveillance system), 10, 46
prisons, secret. *See* secret prisons
private contractors and military. *See* corporate-military complex
privatization, 7, 15, 80, 81, 83
Project for the New American Century (PNAC), 40
Pruitt, Gary, 32, 63
public employees as whistleblowers. *See* whistleblowers
public opinion, American, 123–24, 143
public opinion, Pakistani, 70
publishing industry, 152
Putin, Vladimir, 67, 68, 72

Qaddafi, Muammar, 102, 118–19
Qatar, 54

Rahman, Gul, 88
Reagan, Ronald, 27, 51, 72, 80, 141
rendition, extralegal, 31, 61, 70, 86, 88, 100
reporting. *See* news media

revenge, 30, 38, 53

robotic aircraft. *See* drones and drone wars

Rodriguez, Jose, Jr., 87–88

Ross, Thomas B., 17–21 passim

Royal Dutch Shell, 139

Rumsfeld, Donald, 23, 41–42, 53–54, 112

Russia, 32–33, 48, 56, 67, 68, 72, 93, 100; drones, 124; as energy state, 148; nuclear weapons, 147; tsarist armies, 77

"Salt Pit" prison, Afghanistan, 88

Sandy Hook Elementary School shooting, 2012, 38, 73

Sanger, David, 48

satellites, 12, 21, 22, 56, 83, 100

"Saudi America," 141, 148

Saudi Arabia, 50–55 passim, 148

Scahill, Jeremy: *Dirty Wars*, 41–42

Scalia, Antonin, 12

Scarborough, Rowan, 41–42

Scheer, Robert, 132

Schmitt, Eric, 119

SEALs, 25, 26

secrecy, 6, 9, 35, 46, 50, 62, 82–85, 96, 158. *See also* classified documents; "covert" (word)

secret military forces. *See* special operations forces

secret prisons, 61, 70, 85, 86, 88, 100, 128–29

security, national. *See* national security

Senate, US. *See* US Senate

Senate Intelligence Committee. *See* US Senate: Intelligence Committee

September 11, 2001, terrorist attacks (9/11), 23, 37–42 passim, 53, 61, 112

Shane, Scott, 131–32

Single Integrated Operational Plan (SIOP), 145

Snowden, Edward, 4, 5, 10, 29–33 passim, 43–49 passim, 62, 106, 107, 157–60 passim; effect on Americans, 114; Greenwald on, 1; as modern-day Nathan Hale, 56–57; NRO budget revealed by, 21–22; Obama response, 13; said to have blood on hands, 63

solar energy, 140, 141

Soltis, Andy, 73

Somalia, 26, 39, 69, 89, 97, 102, 112, 119, 133

Soviet Union, 11, 30, 33, 41, 51–52, 111; demise, 22–23, 52, 91–94 passim, 115; nuclear weapons in, 145–46; in Orwell, 110; Vietnam War, 118. *See also* Cold War

special operations forces, 24–26 passim, 39, 96–99 passim, 117, 130

Stalin, Joseph, 72

State Department. *See* US Department of State

Stevens, Christopher, 119

Sudan, 124

suicide, 37–38, 77, 116

suicide bombers, 25, 75, 101, 118. *See also* September 11, 2001, terrorist attacks (9/11)

"superpower" (word), 91

Supreme Court. *See* US Supreme Court

Suskind, Ron, 38

suspects, extralegal rendition of. *See* rendition, extralegal

Syria, 67, 68, 69, 101, 113, 115, 120

Taliban, 36, 52, 75, 103

telephone records and monitoring. *See* phone records and monitoring

television, 26, 150, 151

"terracide," 137–40

terrorism, 38, 52–53, 137, 140. *See also* September 11, 2001, terrorist attacks (9/11)

think tanks, 5, 40, 112, 138, 148

tobacco industry, 139, 142, 148

Tocqueville, Alexis de, 72

"Top Secret America" (Priest and Arkin), 14, 22

torture, 31, 70, 71, 85, 86–90 passim, 134

totalitarianism, 11, 34, 160

tripartite government, 3, 13, 65

triumphalism, 115–18 passim

Truman, Harry, 129
truth, 64–65. *See also* lies and lying; secrecy
Turkey, 93, 117
Turse, Nick, 98

Udall, Mark, 14
underground newspapers, 77, 154
"unipolar world," 91–95, 100, 110, 115–18
United Kingdom, 44, 110, 111, 147
United Nations, 44–45, 68, 114
"unmanned aerial vehicles." *See* drones and drone wars
US Air Force, 82, 89, 99, 116, 146–47
US citizens, US assassination of, 35, 51, 85, 89, 130
US Congress, 14, 19, 34, 49, 64–65, 82, 84, 129; oversight, 65, 81, 131; perjury before, 89–90. *See also* US Senate
US Constitution, 10, 65, 133–34
US Department of Defense, 23–24, 120, 130. *See also* military spending
US Department of Homeland Security (DHS), 3, 39, 121
US Department of Justice, 32, 85–89 passim, 130, 134
US Department of State, 63, 71, 130, 134
US military bases. *See* military bases
US Navy, 8, 70, 98. *See also* SEALs
US public opinion. *See* public opinion
USS *Cole*, 52–53
US Senate, 14, 24, 67, 84, 89; Intelligence Committee, 55, 64, 84, 87
USSR. *See* Soviet Union
US Supreme Court, 12, 34, 49, 84–85

vehicular deaths, 37–38
vengeance. *See* revenge
Vietnam War, 26, 51, 77–81 passim, 115, 118, 132
volunteer military forces, 78–81 passim

Waldman, Paul, 49
war as religion, 134
"war on terror." *See* Global War on Terror

(GWOT)
war reporting, 80
Washington Post, 29, 50
Washington's China (Peck), 40–41
waterboarding, 86, 87
weapons, hypersonic. *See* hypersonic weapons
weapons industry, 8. *See also* arms trade
weapons of mass destruction (WMD), 41–42. *See also* chemical weapons; nuclear weapons
wedding parties as target of US drone strikes, 72–76 passim
whistleblowers, 29–33, 46, 56–59 passim, 64, 87, 90, 106–7, 157–61; definition, 62; said to have blood on hands, 63. *See also* Manning, Chelsea and Snowden, Edward
Whitlock, Craig, 119
Whitman, Walt, 149
WikiLeaks, 63
wiretapping, 33
Wise, David, 17–21 passim
Wolfowitz, Paul, 112
Woodward, Bob, 132–33
World War II, 47
Wyden, Ron, 14, 89

Yemen, 39, 51–55 passim, 69–74 passim, 97, 101, 135; al-Qaeda in, 5, 36, 51; drone strikes on, 26, 51, 72–74, 89, 119, 123, 130–33 passim
Yugoslavia, 112

Zero Dark Thirty, 26
Zubaydah, Abu, 87

ABOUT TOM ENGELHARDT

Tom Engelhardt created and runs the TomDispatch.com website, a project of the Nation Institute, where he is a fellow. He is the author of *The American Way of War* and *The United States of Fear*, both published by Haymarket Books, a highly praised history of American triumphalism in the cold war, *The End of Victory Culture*, and a novel, *The Last Days of Publishing*. Many of his TomDispatch interviews were collected in *Mission Unaccomplished: TomDispatch Interviews with American Iconoclasts and Dissenters*. With Nick Turse, he has written *Terminator Planet: The First History of Drone Warfare, 2001–2050*. He also edited *The World According to TomDispatch: America in the New Age of Empire*, a collection of pieces from his site that functions as an alternative history of the mad Bush years. TomDispatch is the sideline that ate his life. Before that he worked as an editor at Pacific News Service in the early 1970s, and, these last four decades, as an editor in book publishing. For fifteen years, he was senior editor at Pantheon Books, where he edited and published award-winning works ranging from Art Spiegelman's *Maus* and John Dower's *War Without Mercy* to Eduardo Galeano's *Memory of Fire* trilogy. He is now Consulting Editor at Metropolitan Books, as well as the cofounder and coeditor of Metropolitan's The American Empire Project, where he has published bestselling works by Chalmers Johnson, Andrew Bacevich, Noam Chomsky, and Nick Turse, among others. Many of the authors whose books he has edited and published over the years now write for TomDispatch.com. For a number of years, he was also a Teaching Fellow at the Graduate School of Journalism at the University of California, Berkeley. He is married to Nancy J. Garrity, a therapist, and has two children, Maggie and Will, and a grandchild, Charlie.

ABOUT TOMDISPATCH.COM

Tom Engelhardt launched TomDispatch.com in November 2001 as an email publication offering commentary and collected articles from the world press. In December 2002, it gained its name, became a project of the Nation Institute, and went online as "a regular antidote to the mainstream media." The site now features three articles a week, all original to the site. These include Engelhardt's regular commentaries, as well as the work of authors ranging from Rebecca Solnit, Bill McKibben, Barbara Ehrenreich, and Michael Klare to Adam Hochschild, Noam Chomsky, Anand Gopal, and Karen J. Greenberg. Nick Turse, who also writes for the site, is its managing editor and research director. Andy Kroll is its associate editor, Erika Eichelberger its social media director, and Christopher Holmes its copyeditor. TomDispatch is intended to introduce readers to voices and perspectives from elsewhere (even when the elsewhere is here). Its mission is to connect some of the global dots regularly left unconnected by the mainstream media and to offer a clearer sense of how this imperial globe of ours actually works.